Capital Mobility and Tax Competition

Capital Mobility and Tax Competition

Clemens Fuest

University of Cologne
Center for Public Economics
Albertus Magnus-Platz
D-50923 Köln, Germany
clemens.fuest@uni-koeln.de

Bernd Huber

University of Munich
Department of Economics
University of Munich, Germany

Jack Mintz

C.D. Howe Institute and
University of Toronto, Canada

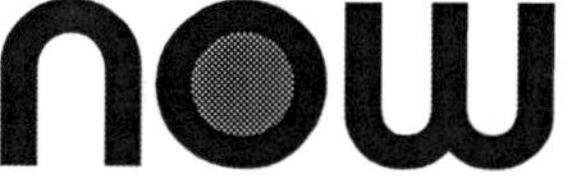

now

the essence of knowledge

Boston – Delft

Foundations and Trends® in Microeconomics

Published, sold and distributed by:
now Publishers Inc.
PO Box 1024
Hanover, MA 02339
USA
Tel. +1 781 871 0245
www.nowpublishers.com
sales@nowpublishers.com

Outside North America:
now Publishers Inc.
PO Box 179
2600 AD Delft
The Netherlands
Tel. +31-6-51115274

A Cataloging-in-Publication record is available from the Library of Congress

Printed on acid-free paper

ISBN: 1-933019-19-0; ISSNs: Paper version 1547-9846;
Electronic version 1547-9854
© 2005 C. Fuest, B. Huber, and J. Mintz

Contents

1

Introduction*

Tax competition and co-ordination is one of the most pressing issues for tax authorities in modern economies. It is also a highly controversial subject. Some argue that tax competition is beneficial by forcing governments to impose efficient tax prices on residents for the provision of public services [83]. In other words, if tax competition leads to less use of source-based taxes (such as taxes on businesses), this would improve the tax policy in competitive economies. Further, some argue that tax competition is also beneficial by limiting the power of governments to levy taxes [14, 52].

Others take a different view. Taxes levied by jurisdictions can impose spillover (or fiscal externality) costs on other jurisdictions [64, 30]. This can take the form of "tax base flight" whereby a jurisdiction's tax results in mobile factors fleeing to low-tax jurisdictions [93]. Alternatively, unco-ordinated taxes can result in "tax exportation" whereby a government shifts the tax burden of financing local public services onto non-residents (e.g. taxes on foreign corporations).

* The authors would like to thank Johannes Becker, Thomas Hemmelgarn and three anonymous referees for very helpful comments on earlier versions of this paper. The usual disclaimer applies.

Therefore, in a world without co-ordinated tax policies, governments choose sub-optimal levels of public services financed by inefficient taxes that are either too high or too low by ignoring spillovers imposed on other jurisdictions.

In recent years, the OECD and the European Union have become increasingly concerned about tax competition. Historically, the OECD developed a model "tax treaty" to limit tax avoidance and reduce "tax exportation" arising from double taxation of income earned by a multinational parent with operations in a capital importing country. A recent OECD project, controversially named "harmful tax competition," is intended to reduce the scope for "tax base flight" externalities by removing incentives to shift tax bases to low-tax jurisdictions. The European Union has not only been looking to implement a "code of conduct" to limit the scope of tax competition but the member countries have also been forced to adopt limitations on tax exportation that discriminates between foreigners and domestic owners of capital.[1] Agreements to limit tax competition have not been easily achieved. Even in the latest round of negotiations, some countries like Luxembourg and the United Kingdom have objected to EU or OECD attempts to limit tax competition.

The purpose of this survey is to draw out the most important issues of un-coordinated tax policy at the international level for cross-border transactions. The discussion focuses on mobile tax bases, specifically in relation to investment and financial transactions. Two important caveats are thus in order. The first is that, even though labour is mobile to some degree, there is still relatively little labour mobility

---

[1] European court cases in recent years induced EU countries to revise their tax systems for the integration of corporate and personal taxes. Most governments only provided a dividend tax credit for domestic shareholders as an offset for corporate taxes paid on income prior to distribution to shareholders. However, a German company operating in Britain argued that the dividend tax credit should also be extended to German shareholders to avoid discrimination against other members of the European Union. The court determined that a tax credit should be paid to shareholders in other European countries. Rather than try to pay credits to foreign shareholders, the United Kingdom changed its existing system to integrate corporate and personal taxes by abolishing the a corporate level tax on distributions and reducing personal taxes on dividends to a level so that the combined corporate (30%) and personal tax rate (10%) on dividends was approximately equal to the top rate on salary and other income (40%). Other countries followed with France recently changing their system in light of these court cases.

at the international level [43]. Thus, we concern ourselves with tax competition in relation to mobile capital and finance.[2] The second is that investment and financial transactions are taxed at the business level and household level. Although there is certainly some significant concern on part of authorities that individual residents can escape taxation on income by investing wealth in low-tax offshore jurisdictions, the most substantial problems arise with respect to business income and financial transactions taxes since most cross-border transactions involve companies and financial intermediaries.

Our main issue for consideration in this survey is whether taxation of income, specifically capital income will survive, how border crossing investment is taxed relative to domestic investment and whether welfare gains can be achieved through international tax coordination. The survey should be seen as complementing related contributions which include Keen [50], Wilson [91], Wellisch [85], Gresik [37], Haufler [39], Wildasin and Wilson [92]. One difference to these surveys is that our paper attempts to derive some of the key results on the taxation of international investment in variants of one model of multinational investment, which we develop in Section 2. Moreover, we put emphasis on the problem of tax competition and financial arbitrage, an issue which is somewhat neglected in the existing surveys.

The outline for the paper is the following. The paper consists of two major parts. The first part (Section 2) deals with the implications of tax competition for national tax policy. Section 2.1 begins with a discussion of some basic results for the optimal taxation of border crossing direct investment. In the following sections, we extend our analysis to include the role of double taxation agreements (Section 2.2), public goods provision (Section 2.3), portfolio investment (Section 2.4) and transfer pricing (Section 2.5). Section 2.6 deals with the role of the financing decisions and financial arbitrage for investment and tax policy under tax competition. The second major part of the paper (Section 3) deals with the problem of tax coordination. We start with the basic idea that tax competition leads to an underprovision of public

---

[2] On fiscal competition with household mobility see Richter and Wellisch [76], Wellisch [85] and Wildasin [87]. Kessler et al. [54] investigate the interaction between capital mobility and household mobility.

goods (Sections 3.1 and 3.2) and then consider the role of residence-based capital income taxes (Section 3.3), labour taxes (Section 3.4), and redistributive income taxation (Section 3.5). Section 3.6 discusses reasons why taxes may be too high rather than too low under tax competition. Finally, Section 3.7 focuses on the problem of regional versus global tax coordination. Section 4 concludes the survey.

2

International Capital Income Taxation and Tax Competition

2.1 How Should Foreign Investment Income be Taxed?

An early analysis of the taxation of foreign investment income is due to Musgrave and Brewer [68] and Musgrave [67]. They argue that a country should tax the income from foreign investment of domestic firms "in order to ensure that further investment is not made if the net foreign return is below the gross return on domestic investment" [67, p. 98]. One way of achieving this is to tax foreign profits at the same rate as domestic profits but let foreign taxes be deducted from the tax base. A formal treatment of this question which leads to the same result can be found in the seminal paper by Feldstein and Hartman [19]. These authors analyse the optimal taxation of capital income resulting from international direct investment. The key result can be derived from a simplified version of their model.

Consider a world of two jurisdictions denoted as the home country and the foreign country. There is a multinational firm that has its headquarters in the home country and produces domestically and abroad. Domestic output is $Y^d = F^d(K^d, L^d)$ and output produced in the foreign country is $Y^f = F^f(K^f, L^f)$, where K and L are capital and labour and the subscripts d and f refer to the home country and the foreign country, respectively. Labour is assumed to be internationally immobile and fixed in supply. The production functions $F^d(K^d, L^d)$ and $F^f(K^f, L^f)$ have the usual neoclassical properties and exhibit constant returns to scale. Moreover, denote by t^d the domestic profit tax rate and by t^f the profit tax rate in the foreign country. The home country owns the entire capital stock $S^d = K^d + K^f$ and S^d is fixed. Assuming that all investment is equity financed, after tax profits of the multinational firm (P) can be expressed as

$$P = (1 - t^d)\left(F^d(K^d, L^d) - w^d L^d\right) + (1 - t^E)\left(F^f(K^f, L^f) - w^f L^f\right)$$
$$(2.1)$$

where w^d and w^f denote the domestic and foreign wage rates,

$$t^E = t^f(1 - a) + t^d \tag{2.2}$$

is the effective tax rate on foreign investment and a is a parameter which captures the treatment of foreign profits and taxes paid in the foreign country by the domestic tax system. For example, $a = t^d$ would imply a deduction system while $a = 1$ would represent the case where foreign taxes are (fully) credited. The profit maximizing investment decision implies

$$(1 - t^d)F_K^d = (1 - t^E)F_K^f, \tag{2.3}$$

that is the firm equates the marginal productivity of capital net of taxes in the two countries. Equation (2.3) thus describes the allocation of the capital stock across countries, given the tax policies of the home and the foreign country.

Feldstein and Hartman concentrate on the tax policy of the capital exporting country and assume that the government pursues the objective of maximizing domestic income including domestic tax revenue. There is no public sector revenue requirement such that tax policy is used exclusively to influence international capital movements. The capital exporting country takes the wage rate w^f and the tax policy of the foreign country as given. Domestic income is

$$F^d(K^d, L^d) + (1 - t^f)\left(F^f(K^f, L^f) - w^f L^f\right). \tag{2.4}$$

For a given t^f, the domestic government can control K^d (and, since $S^d = K^d + K^f$ also K^f), using its tax instruments t^d and a. The policy which maximizes domestic income implies

$$F_K^d = (1 - t^f)F_K^f. \tag{2.5}$$

The explanation for this result is that, at the optimum, the contribution to domestic income of a marginal unit of capital invested domestically, including the tax revenue it generates, should equal the marginal productivity of capital invested abroad, net of foreign taxes, as already stated by Musgrave [67]. The implication of (2.5) for domestic tax policy is easily derived by substituting (2.5) and (2.2) into (2.3), which yields $a = t^d$. The home country will thus fully tax repatriated profits but allow the multinational to deduct taxes paid abroad from the tax base (full taxation after deduction).

One important assumption made in the Feldstein–Hartman model is that countries face no legal constraints in the taxation of income from foreign investment. While this is a useful benchmark case for theoretical analysis, empirical tax policy vis-à-vis multinational firms is usually constrained by double taxation agreements. This is why a large part of the literature on the taxation of international direct investment takes into account the rules stipulated in double taxation agreements.

2.2 Tax Competition and Double Taxation Agreements

Most existing double taxation agreements follow the OECD Double Taxation Convention [72]. According to this model treaty, countries are allowed to tax the income from foreign investment of their multinational firms either according to the credit system or the exemption system. Under the exemption system, foreign profits are exempt from domestic taxation. As a result, capital income is effectively taxed according to the source principle. If the exemption system is applied, after tax profits of the multinational firm are

$$P = (1 - t^d)\left(F^d(K^d, L^d) - w^d L^d\right) + (1 - t^f)\left(F^f(K^f, L^f) - w^f L^f\right) \tag{2.6}$$

and the firm's profit maximizing investment decision now implies

$$(1 - t^d)F_K^d = (1 - t^f)F_K^f. \tag{2.7}$$

What is the optimal tax policy under the exemption system? Overall income of the capital exporting country is again given by (2.4). Maximizing (2.4) over t^d yields

$$\left(F_K^d - (1 - t^f)F_K^f \right) K_{t^d}^d - (1 - t^f)w_{t^d}^f L^f = 0. \tag{2.8}$$

If the capital exporting country takes the wage rate in the capital importing country as given, i.e. it assumes $w_{t^d}^f = 0$, (2.7) and (2.8) imply $t^d = 0$. Things are different if the government of the capital exporting country takes into account that an increase in domestic taxation drives up foreign wages because it encourages foreign investment, i.e. $w_{t^d}^f > 0$. In this case, equation (2.8) implies $t^d < 0$. The capital exporting country subsidizes domestic investment. Subsidizing domestic investment allows the capital exporting country to use its market power in the foreign labor market. Accordingly, it is straightforward to show that the optimal tax policy of the capital importing country will imply $t^f = 0$ if it takes the marginal productivity of capital in the capital exporting country, F_K^d, as given. However, if it takes into account that the reduction in capital imports caused by an increase in t^f drives down F_K^d, it will set $t^f > 0$. In this case, the capital importing country acts as a monopsonist in the international capital market.[1]

As an alternative to the exemption system, the OECD Double Taxation Convention allows countries to tax international investment income according to the tax credit system. Under this system, both domestic and foreign profits are subject to domestic taxation. But taxes on foreign profits paid abroad are credited against domestic taxes on foreign profits. The maximum credit is, however, the domestic tax liability on foreign profits, i.e. the domestic government does not fully refund foreign taxes if the foreign tax rate is higher than the domestic one. After tax profits can then be written as

$$P = (1 - t^d)\left(F^d(K^d, L^d) - w^d L^d \right)$$
$$+ (1 - \max[t^d, t^f])\left(F^f(K^f, L^f) - w^f L^f \right). \tag{2.9}$$

---

[1] In a similar way, countries may employ import and export tariffs in order to exploit market power in international trade, see e.g. Dixit [13].

An important question in the literature on tax policy under the foreign tax credit system is whether, from a worldwide perspective, it leads to more efficient outcomes than the deduction system. In the earlier literature [67], the full taxation after deduction system is usually seen as inefficient from a global point of view because it gives rise to a double taxation of income from international investment and thus discriminates foreign relative to domestic investment. Under the credit system, in contrast, no such double taxation occurs. For given tax rates, the deduction system is thus less favourable to trade in capital than the credit system.

However, this does not mean that the foreign tax credit system necessarily leads to more efficient outcomes. Bond and Samuelson [4] use a variant of the Feldstein–Hartman model to analyse the outcome of tax competition under the foreign tax credit system. It turns out that, if one takes into account that the level of tax rates depends on system of double taxation relief, the bias against trade in capital is much worse under the credit system.[2]

The anti trade bias of the credit system can be demonstrated using the model introduced above. The foreign tax credit system implies that the effective tax rate on foreign investment is $t^E = \max[t^{df}, t^f]$, where t^{df} now denotes the domestic tax rate on corporate income from foreign investment. The tax rate on domestic profits (t^d) is assumed to be zero. The profits of the multinational firm are $F^d(K^d, L^d) - w^d L^d + (1 - \max[t^{df}, t^f])\left(F^f(K^f, L^f) - w^f L^f\right)$. The firm's optimal investment behaviour is thus determined by the condition

$$F_K^d = (1 - \max[t^{df}, t^F])F_K^f. \tag{2.10}$$

The optimal level of employment in the foreign country (L^f) satisfies the standard marginal productivity condition $F_L^i = w^i$, $i = d, f$. The analysis thus assumes that firms take the factor prices w^d and w^f as given.

Under tax competition, the capital exporting and the capital importing country simultaneously set their tax rates to maximize domestic income. Consider first the capital importing country. Note

---

[2] A similar result is derived by Oakland and Xu [70].

that, if $t^f < t^{df}$, raising t^f increases tax revenue in the capital importing country but leaves the capital stock K^f unchanged. Therefore, the capital importing country will always set $t^f \geq t^{df}$. What about the capital exporting country? For the capital exporting country, it is also suboptimal to choose a lower tax rate than the capital importing country. Effectively, if $t^{df} < t^f$, the credit system is equivalent to the exemption system and the level of t^{df} plays no role. So the question arises whether the domestic country would want to raise t^{df} above t^f. It turns out that this is the case if and only if the volume of capital exports K^f affects the wage rate in the capital importing country. National income of the capital exporting country is $F^d(K^d, L^d) + (1 - t^f)\left(F^f(K^f, L^f) - w^f L^f\right)$. Using $S^d - K^d = K^f$ and the conditions for the firm's optimal investment and employment decisions, the effect of a marginal increase of t^{df} on domestic welfare welfare, evaluated at $t^{df} = t^f$, can be written as

$$-(1 - t^f)w^f_{t_{df}}L^f = (1 - t^f)K^f F^f_{KK}K^f_{t_{df}} > 0. \tag{2.11}$$

It thus turns out that the capital exporting country will always want to set $t^{df} > t^f$. As equation (2.11) shows, the reason for the capital exporting country to raise its tax rate above that of the capital importing country is that the wage rate w^f in the foreign country declines if t^{df} increases (and K^f declines). Since the capital exporting firms are assumed to take w^f as given, there is an incentive to use tax policy as an instrument of exploiting market power vis-à-vis the capital importing country. Of course, $t^{df} > t^f$ cannot hold in equilibrium because the optimal tax policy of the capital importing country implies $t^f \geq t^{df}$. This implies that the only equilibrium under the foreign tax credit system is an equilibrium where tax rates are so high that border crossing investment vanishes.

A critical assumption underlying the above analysis is that countries may levy different tax rates on income from foreign and domestic investment. The OECD Double Taxation Convention (1997)[3] forbids this type of discrimination.[4] Many contributions to the literature therefore rule out the possibility of raising different tax rates on domestic

---

[3] For an economic analysis of the OECD double taxation convention see Mintz and Tulkens [65].

and foreign source income [9, 27, 32, 49]. In our model, this implies $t^{df} = t^d$. So let t^d be the uniform tax rate on domestic and foreign source income of the capital exporting country. Under this assumption, it can be shown that tax competition under the credit system leads to an equilibrium with positive international capital flows.

To see this, note first that the capital importing country will pursue the same policy, i.e. it will always set $t^f \geq t^d$. In contrast, the policy of the capital exporting country changes. It is an immediate implication of nondiscrimination that the capital exporting country cannnot increase its welfare by raising t^d above t^f. The reason is that, if $t^d \geq t^f$, an increase in t^d does not affect the capital allocation. This implies that the terms of trade effect which drives the result in Bond and Samuelson [4] cannot occur here. The tax increase only shifts income from the firm owners to the government of the capital exporting country. This has no effect on welfare. So the next question is whether the capital exporting country wants to reduce t^d below t^f. If $t^d < t^f$, a reduction in t^d reduces the tax burden on domestic investment but leaves the tax burden on foreign investment unchanged. For $t^d < t^f$ we therefore have $K^d_{t^d} < 0$. This implies that the capital exporting country may still strategically reduce the supply of capital to the foreign country by reducing t^d. However, this comes at the cost of distorting domestic investment. If $t^d < t^f$, the effect of a marginal increase in t^d on domestic income is

$$ t^d F^d_K K^d_{t^d} - (1 - t^f) w^f_{t^d} L^f. \tag{2.12} $$

Equation (2.12) implies that the capital exporting country will subsidise domestic investment in equilibrium because, if $t^d > 0$, both terms in (2.12) are negative. In contrast, if $t^d < 0$, the first term in (2.12) is positive and captures the cost of the subsidy, which is a distortion of domestic investment.[5] The second term is negative and stands for the

---

[4] In practice, though, many countries do discriminate between domestic and foreign income; see Hines [44].

[5] Janeba [49, p. 318] finds that the home country will choose a zero tax rate. This is because he assumes that tax rates cannot be negative (see [49, p. 314]).

marginal benefit of the subsidy, which is the reduction in the foreign wage. Note that, if the capital exporting country is assumed to be small, i.e. it takes w^f as given, it will simply set $t^d = 0$.

What is the response of the capital importing country? National income of the capital importing country can be written as $F^f(K^f, L^f) - (1 - t^f)K^f F_K^f$. Maximizing this expression over t^f immediately leads to the result that the capital importing country will set $t^f = 0$ if it is small, i.e. it takes the required return to investment $(1 - t^d)F_K^d$ as given. If it is large, it takes into account that a relocation of capital to the capital exporting country lowers the required rate of return. In this case, it exploits its market power and sets $t^f > 0$. The assumption of nondiscrimination between corporate taxes on domestic and foreign profits thus leads to the finding that capital exporting countries will subsidize domestic investment in order to improve their terms of trade in capital whereas large capital importing countries will tax capital for the same reason (see, for instance, [78]). The result that tax credits lead to vanishing trade in capital does not hold anymore. So an important policy conclusion emerging from the discussion in this section is that nondiscrimination clauses in international tax treaties may help to avoid an excessive taxation of international direct investment.

What is the optimal tax policy of the two countries under the exemption system and the deduction system? The exemption system is equivalent to the tax credit system if $t^d < t^f$. Therefore, the equilibrium for the tax credit system described above is also an equilibrium under the exemption system. Janeba [49] shows that these two tax regimes lead to the same allocation if there is a nonnegativity constraint on tax rates, and our analysis shows that the result also holds if we do allow tax rates to be negative (the possibility of negative effective tax rates on FDI is explored in the section on financial arbitrage when we discuss tax planning and debt finance). What happens under the deduction system? In this case, the home country cannot improve its terms of trade because a change in t^d does not affect the capital allocation. Therefore, a change in t^d does not affect the welfare of the home country, and the optimal tax rate is undetermined. The capital importing country again taxes domestic investment in order to improve its term of trade if it is large, but the equilibrium capital allocation is now different.[6]

2.3 The Role of Public Goods Provision

In the literature discussed so far, corporate income taxes essentially have the function to influence the terms of trade in capital. While this may well be a relevant factor in tax policy decisions in some cases, it cannot explain corporate tax policy in general. If terms of trade considerations generally determined corporate tax policy, one would expect that tax policy depends on whether countries are net capital exporters or capital importers. This is not consistent with the observed patterns of tax policy [32]. Moreover, most countries are unlikely to have significant market power in international capital markets.[7]

Of course, the main reason for levying taxes in general is that governments have to finance their expenditure on publicly provided goods. However, this does not necessarily imply that corporate income taxes will be used. In fact, a well known result of optimal tax theory states that a small open economy should not levy source-based capital taxes if other tax instruments such as, for instance, labour taxes, are available [11, 31]. In the light of this theoretical finding, the empirical observation that countries do levy corporate income taxes is puzzling. Gordon [32] discusses possible explanations for this puzzle. He argues that, in a world where public goods have to be financed via distortionary taxes, positive corporate income taxes may be explained by the existence of foreign tax credits.

Gordon's results can be derived in an extended version of the model used in the preceding sections. Let the utility function of the representative household residing in the capital exporting country be $W^d = M(C^d) + H(G^d)$ where C^d and G^d denote private and public consumption and $M(\cdot)$ and $H(\cdot)$ are concave functions with the usual

---

[6] In Janeba [49], the deduction system also leads to the same allocation as the two other tax regimes. In our model, the deduction system leads to a different allocation because we do not assume that tax rates cannot be negative.

[7] Gordon and Varian [35] develop a model where countries are small but have specific risk characteristics, this is also a source of market power. However, the optimal tax policy implies that countries would subsidise rather than tax domestic investment.

properties. The government may finance G via two tax instruments: the corporate income tax and a tax on the income of the fixed factor L^d. Residence-based taxes on capital income levied at the household level are ruled out. We assume further that the income of the fixed factor is taxed at a rate of 100%. It is well known that, if there are untaxed rents, it is optimal to levy positive source-based capital taxes, so that it would not be surprising to find positive corporate income taxes if rent taxation is restricted. For the capital importing country, we make the same assumptions.[8]

What is the equilibrium tax policy emerging under tax competition? Consider first the capital importing country. In order to exclude terms of trade considerations from the analysis, Gordon assumes that the government takes the required rate of return for capital imports $(1 - t^d) \times F_K^d$ as given. It turns out that the capital importing country will never set $t^f < t^d$ because, if $t^f < t^d$, it can always raise tax revenue by increasing t^f without changing domestic investment. It is also easy to show that the capital importing country will not raise t^f above t^d (provided that $t^d \geq 0$) because this would distort investment and the increase in corporate tax revenue would be smaller than the decline in rent tax revenue. The capital importing country thus always sets $t^f = t^d$.

What is the optimal tax policy of the capital exporting country? The budget constraint of the private household in the capital exporting country is

$$C^d = (1 - t^d)F_K^d K^d + (1 - \max[t^d, t^f])F_K^f K^f \qquad (2.13)$$

and the government's budget is

$$G^d = F^d(K^d, L^d) - (1 - t^d)F_K^d K^d + \max[t^d - t^f, 0]F_K^f K^f. \qquad (2.14)$$

The government of the capital exporting country also takes the rate of return on exported capital $(1 - t^f)F_K^f$ as given. Consider first the case with $t^d < t^f$. In this case, the effect of a marginal increase in t^d on domestic welfare is $H_G t^d F_K^d K_{t^d}^d$ which is negative

---

[8] On the optimal taxation of capital in the presence of untaxed rents, see Horst [45] and Keen and Piekkola [51]. By assumption, the household residing in the capital importing country has no capital income. The government may therefore want to pay transfers to the household. Our results are not affected by this issue.

for $t^d > 0$, so that the only symmetric pure strategy equilibrium can be $t^f = t^d = 0$. But if $t^f = t^d$, a marginal increase in t^d reduces the after tax rate of return on investment in both countries but leaves the capital allocation unaffected. The effect on domestic welfare is $\left(F_K^d K^d + F_K^f K^f\right)(H_G - M_C) > 0$. For a given corporate tax rate in the capital importing country, an increase in t^d is equivalent to an increase in a residence-based tax on capital income. If $H_G > M_C$, the government of the capital exporting country will want to levy such a tax. Of course, $t^d > t^f$ cannot be an equilibrium since the capital importing country always wants to set $t^f = t^d$. It thus turns out that no Nash equilibrium in pure strategies exists. One may note that this result emerges despite the assumption that the capital exporting country must set a uniform corporate income tax rate for domestic and foreign profits.

Thus, the conclusion emerging from the above analysis is that, if both countries move simultaneously and take the tax rate of the other country as given, tax credits cannot explain the existence of positive corporate income taxes. As a second step, Gordon [32] therefore considers the case where the capital exporting country acts as a Stackelberg leader, i.e. it takes into account that the capital importing country will always set $t^f = t^d$. In this case, the effect of a marginal increase in t^d on the government's objective function is $F_K^d K^d (H_G - M_C) - F_K^f K^f M_C$. The first term is positive if $H_G > U_C$, which reflects that welfare increases as income is transferred from the private to the public sector. The second term is negative and captures the effect of the increase in the foreign tax rate. This implies that an equilibrium with positive corporate taxes is possible. Gordon [32] explains this as follows: "From the investor's perspective, it is as if the country were using a residence-based tax. The government, however, cedes the tax revenue on capital exports to the other governments ... reducing the attractiveness of the tax relative to a true residence-based tax ... The main conclusion, however, is that the tax can survive in equilibrium." (pp. 1170–71).

It thus turns out that corporate income taxes may survive under tax competition if income from foreign investment is taxed according to the foreign tax credit system. However, this result emerges in Gordon's analysis only under quite restrictive assumptions. Firstly, the capital exporting country must act as a Stackelberg leader. Secondly, it is assumed that households can only invest abroad via the multinational firm. This assumption is problematic because it excludes, for instance, international portfolio investment of domestic households. In fact, one reason why residence-based taxes on capital income are difficult to implement is that private households may avoid these taxes by investing their savings in bank accounts abroad. Another is simply the difficulty of applying taxes on gross interest receipts earned by international financial traders who pay tax only on the net yield received from financial transactions and derivatives. So a more complete picture of international capital market integration would require the possibility of international portfolio investment by households and the possibility of firms to finance their investment via the international capital market.

2.4 Tax Competition with Multinational Firms and Portfolio Investment

In the literature, there are some papers analyzing tax policy in the presence of both multinational firms and portfolio investment [12, 27, 66]. What does the introduction of portfolio investment change? If the model discussed in the preceding section is extended by portfolio investment, the result that no Nash equilibrium exists under the tax credit system, given that both countries set their tax rates simultaneously, vanishes. To see why, assume that the two countries are linked by an international capital market, where households may invest their savings at the interest rate r. Firms also finance their investment via the international capital market. Each individual country takes the interest rate r as given.[9]

The possibility of international portfolio investment by private households raises the question how this investment is taxed. A large part of the literature assumes that income from portfolio investment accruing to private households is untaxed. This assumption is usually

---

[9] Given that there are only two countries, this assumption seems artificial. It allows us to rule out an impact of terms of trade effects on the optimal tax policy and to focus on the role of double taxation agreements.

justified by pointing out that residence-based capital income taxes can easily be avoided by holding bank accounts abroad.

Under these assumptions, firms have to offer private investors an after tax return to capital which is equal to r. The investment behavior of the multinational firm follows from maximizing

$$P = (1 - t^d)\left(F^d(K^d, L^d) - w^d L^d\right)$$
$$+ (1 - t^E)\left(F^f(K^f, L^f) - w^f L^f\right) - r(K^d + K^f) \qquad (2.15)$$

over K^d and K^f. The optimal levels of K^d and K^f are therefore given by $(1 - t^d)F_K^d = r$ and $(1 - t^E)F_K^f = r$. If we maintain the assumption that the income of the fixed factor accrues to the government, private consumption in the capital exporting country is simply $C^d = rS^d$, where S^d is the household's endownment with capital.

How does the possibility of portfolio investment by private households affect tax policy? If the interest rate r is given, tax policy does not affect private consumption. The optimal policy thus boils down to maximizing public goods provision.[10] Consider first the case of the exemption system, which means $t^E = t^f$. In this case, the firms optimal investment policy implies $K_{t^d}^d < 0, K_{t^f}^d = 0$ and $K_{t^f}^f < 0,\ K_{t^d}^f = 0$. Public consumption of the capital exporting country is given by

$$G^d = F^d(K^d, L^d) - rK^d \qquad (2.16)$$

Maximizing (2.16) over t^d yields $t^d = 0$, i.e. the optimal tax is zero. Accordingly, public consumption in the capital importing country is $G^f = F^f(K^f, L^f) - rK^f$, and the optimal corporate tax is also zero. It thus turns out that the optimal capital income taxes under the exemption system are zero, as in the model without portfolio investment.

Does this result change if the tax credit system applies? In this case, domestic and foreign investment of the multinational firm are given by the first order conditions $(1 - t^d)F_K^d = r$ and $(1 - \max[t^d, t^f])F_K^f = r$. Note that this implies $K_{t^f}^f < 0,\ K_{t^d}^f = 0$ if $t^f \geq t^d$. But if $t^f < t^d$, we

---

[10] This is true only as along as the marginal utility of public consumption is not lower than the marginal utility of private consumption, i.e. $H_G > M_C$. If H_G approaches M_C, the government will use excess tax revenue to pay lump sum transfers to the households, rather than supplying more public goods.

have $K^f_{t^f} = 0$, $K^f_{t^d} < 0$. The objective function of the capital importing country is given by $G^f = F^f(K^f, L^f) - rK^f + t^f F^f_K K^f$. If $t^f < t^d$, an increase in t^f always increases tax revenue without reducing investment in the foreign country. Therefore, the capital importing country will always set $t^f = t^d$, as in the model without portfolio investment.

Can $t^f = t^d$ be an equilibrium? Under the tax credit system, the government budget constraint of the capital exporting country is given by

$$G^d = F^d(K^d, L^d) - (1 - t^d)F^d_K K^d + \max[t^d - t^f, 0]F^f_K K^f. \quad (2.17)$$

The f.o.c. for the optimal tax policy, evaluated for $t^f = t^d$, can be written as

$$t^d F^d_K K^d_{t^d} + F^f_K K^f = 0. \quad (2.18)$$

The first term on the left-hand side of (2.18) is negative if $t^d > 0$ and the second term is positive. It thus turns out that a Nash equilibrium in pure strategies with $t^f = t^d > 0$ exists (see the discussion in [27]) and tax credits do explain the existence of positive corporate tax rates even if both countries move simultaneously.

How can we explain the difference to the model without portfolio investment by private households, discussed in Section 2.3? In the model without portfolio investment, an increase in t^d (departing from $t^f = t^d$) does not affect investment since there is no untaxed asset.[11] In contrast, in the presence of untaxed portfolio investment, an increase in t^d does distort investment, both domestic and foreign. The distortion in domestic investment acts as a break on the incentives to raise t^d. So it turns out that, if taxes on domestic and foreign corporate profits are nondiscriminatory,[12] if households are allowed to invest abroad through other channels than domestic firms, and if the income from this investment cannot be taxed, the existence of tax credits and multinational firms can explain the observation that even small open economies levy positive corporate income taxes. Fuest and Huber [27] also show that

---

[11] In Gordon's [32] model, the level of investment changes because savings respond to the decline in the after tax return to savings. In the simpler model used here, investment does not change since savings are fixed.

[12] One may note that, if the capital exporting country was allowed to tax foreign and domestic profits at different rates, the Bond–Samuelson–Gordon result would reappear.

positive corporate tax rates emerge under the deduction system and in the asymmetric case where one group of countries applies the tax credit system and another group applies the exemption system.

One should note, though, that the above result is derived in a model where foreign profits can only be repatriated at one point in time. In a multi-period context, the result only holds if foreign investment income is taxed by the domestic country upon accrual or if multinational firms repatriate their profits in each period. In practice, most countries with tax credit systems tax foreign profits only when they are repatriated. Since corporate taxes in the host country have to be paid immediately whereas tax credits are only available when profits are repatriated, it is clear that corporate income taxes of the host country do affect the cost of capital and, hence, investment behaviour. The host country will therefore not be able to set $t^f = t^d > 0$ without distorting capital imports. As Gordon [33, p. 29] notes, given that countries usually tax foreign profits only when they are repatriated, the existence of tax credits would encourage the use of withholding taxes for dividend distributions rather than the use of corporate income taxes.[13] Moreover, Altshuler and Gruber [1] show that there are many ways in which companies can achieve the equivalent of repatriation, i.e. transferring cash to the parent, without having to pay repatriation taxes. For instance, subsidiaries from low tax countries may invest in passive assets, which the parent can borrow against, or the low tax subsidiary may invest in other subsidiaries located in high tax countries. These subsidiaries may transfer their profits to the parent company.

Another simplifying assumption made in the above analysis is that the multinational firm only invests in one foreign country. If it invests in more than one foreign country, it may use excess credits for profits generated in high tax countries to shelter profits repatriated from low tax countries. If this "averaging" allows multinational firms to entirely avoid domestic taxation of foreign profits, the domestic corporate income tax becomes a tax on domestic investment only. As mentioned above, it is inefficient for a small open economy to have such a tax.

---

[13] Altshuler and Newlon [2] discuss how withholding taxes and corporate income taxes together influence the cost of capital of foreign direct investment.

2.5   Transfer Prices and International Income Shifting

In the literature discussed so far, it has been assumed that it is possible for the government to observe the location where the income of multinational firms is generated, i.e. that it is possible to distinguish clearly between domestic and foreign source income. This assumption is problematic for a number of reasons. One important issue is that, in most multinational firms, there is a significant amount of intra firm trade. When a multinational parent provides a service or sells a non-marketed good to a foreign subsidiary, a transfer price has to be charged. If market prices are not available, multinational firms may distort the transfer price from the price that would be charged by two independent businesses in order to shift taxable income to the jurisdiction where taxes are lower.[14] Another method commonly used by multinationals that allows profits to be shifted is to move debt to the high-tax jurisdiction, a topic that we will discuss more fully in the next section on finance. Of course, transfer pricing and other options give rise to tax savings only if income generated abroad escapes domestic taxation. This is the case, for instance, if the home country applies the exemption system or, to a somewhat lesser extent, if the home country operates a tax credit system with deferral. There is a large literature studying the empirical evidence for transfer pricing behavior. This literature confirms that income shifting through transfer prices and other means are used extensively as a way of avoiding taxes.[15]

More specifically, the transfer pricing problem raises several policy issues. Firstly, governments may take the manipulation of transfer prices as given and adjust their tax policy accordingly. Secondly, governments may impose transfer pricing rules in order to prevent profit shifting. The first issue is analysed in Gordon and MacKie-Mason [29] and in Haufler and Schelderup [40]. Gordon and MacKie-Mason [29] consider a model of a small open economy, where individuals spend part of their time working as employees and the rest working as

---

[14] As Slemrod [80, p. 484] puts it, "... the *location* of the income of an integrated global enterprise is a conceptual nightmare."

[15] It is conceptually difficult to distinguish transfer pricing and other means of income shifting in empirical studies. The empirical literature on international income shifting is surveyed in Gresik [37, pp. 808–811]

entrepreneurs. Profits of entrepreneurs are taxed as corporate income. The government may levy taxes on labor income, on corporate income, and an additional tax on inputs. The input tax distorts the firm's production decisions. In a world where all corporations are owned by domestic households, and these corporations do not have foreign subsidiaries, the optimal tax rate on corporate income is the same as the labor income tax, and the government would not want to use the distortionary input tax.

How does the optimal tax policy change if multinational firms take over domestic firms, so that these firms may use transfer prices to shift profits to low tax countries? In this case, the government reduces the corporate tax rate below the labor tax rate in order to prevent income shifting. Moreover, the optimal distortionary input tax is now positive. The use of distortionary input taxes prevents an excessive shift of working time into entrepreneurial activity and allows to tax the income of entrepreneurs without creating incentives for income shifting through transfer pricing.

Haufler and Schjelderup [40] consider a model of tax competition among small open economies and focus on the interaction between the corporate tax rate and the tax base. If the possibility of transfer price manipulation by multinational firms is ruled out, the optimal corporate tax policy allows for a full deduction of the costs of capital, i.e, the corporate income tax is a cash flow tax which implies that the marginal tax burden on domestic investment is zero. The authors then allow firms to manipulate transfer prices in order to shift income to low tax jurisdictions. In this case, countries reduce their profit tax rates in order to limit profit shifting to low tax countries. The opportunity of profit shifting thus acts as a restriction on profit taxation. In the presence of such a restriction, it is optimal to distort the investment decision. The tax on the marginal investment acts as a substitute for the restricted profit tax.

Elitzur and Mintz [18] analyse the issue of transfer price setting by the government. They consider a model where a multinational parent sells a non-marketed good to a foreign subsidiary which is run by a local management partner. The profit of the foreign subsidiary is a function of the manager's effort, which cannot be observed by the parent. The parent thus faces a principal-agent problem and offers a compensation to the manager which contains a share in the subsidiary's profits. This profit also depends on the transfer price charged by the parent for the good sold to the subsidiary. Since the government is assumed not to observe the actual transfer price, it has to set a transfer price for tax purposes. This is done on the basis of average profitability the government observes in similar activities. Given this transfer price and the behaviour of the parent and the management partner, countries choose positive corporate income tax rates. They do so because part of the tax burden is borne by the other country. In this framework, it turns out that governments use unilateral transfer pricing regulations as an instrument to shift tax revenue from the foreign country to the home country (see also [61] and [74]).

Konrad and Lommerud [57] also discuss transfer price setting by the government but emphasize that governments may try to extract information from firms about the "true" costs of goods traded within multinational firms by offering incentive compatible contracts. They consider a model where firms may shift income across borders because the government of the host country cannot observe the true production costs of an input to local production bought from the parent company, which resides abroad. There are two types of firms which differ in the true cost of the imported input. The optimal transfer price policy has to set incentives for firms to reveal their type. Thus, low cost firms earn an information rent. Konrad and Lommerud also mention that the possibility of income shifting, which arises due to informational asymmetries between firms and governments may be an advantage for countries if they cannot commit to non-confiscatory taxation.

2.6   The Financial Structure of Firms

2.6.1   The Exemption System

Another complication for the allocation of a firm's income to a location is due to the possibility of changing a firm's financial structure. We have assumed so far that all investment is equity financed. This neglects that firms may at least partly finance their investment via debt. Given that firms may deduct the interest payments on debt from the corporate tax base, they may shift income from one country to another simply by changing the financial structure of the firm. For example, the domestic firm may borrow funds and use them to increase the equity of a subsidiary. This has important implications for the cost of capital faced by multinational firms. As in the case of transfer pricing, the tax incentives to change the financial structure of firms depend, among other things, on the system for the taxation of foreign profits in the multinational firm of the home country. To begin, we consider the impact of taxes in the presence of the exemption system so that a taxpayer only pays corporate income taxes to the government where income is earned at source. In the next section, the more complicated foreign tax credit regimes are considered.

As in the preceding sections, we consider a multinational firm with two sources of profits in two countries, the domestic country (with superscript d) and the foreign country (with superscript f). Since this section focuses on the effects of financing decisions on a multinational firm's cost of capital and the shifting of profits across borders, we now suppress the fixed factor L and assume that any rents carned by this factor accrue as corporate income. The main difference to the models analysed so far, though, is that we now allow for debt financing. To keep things simple, we assume that the interest rate is identical for domestic and foreign debt and we abstract from personal income taxes and source taxes on interest or dividend payments. Interest payments on debt are deductible from the corporate tax base. The multinational firm's profits are given by

$$P = (1 - t^d)\left(F^d(K^d) - rB^d\right) + (1 - t^f)\left(F^f(K^f) - rB^f\right) \quad (2.19)$$

where B^d and B^f denote domestic and foreign debt. The question of how the financial structure of firms is determined in general is a complicated issue which cannot be discussed at length here. For our purposes, it is sufficient to simply assume that the firm finances a share β of its overall investment through debt. The firm thus faces the financing constraint

$$B^f + B^d = \beta(K^d + K^f). \quad (2.20)$$

The tax arbitrage among businesses facing differing corporate tax rates can be seen from equation (2.19). For instance, a multinational can finance all of its capital from one country and transfer equity funds to the other. It would do so if there are tax benefits from this strategy. If the corporate tax rate in the foreign country is less than the home country tax rate $(t^f < t^d)$, then it is obvious that the optimal financial policy is to finance investment with borrowing in the home country and a transfer of equity to the foreign country so that $B^d = \beta(K^d + K^f)$. The cost of capital for multinational investment in the each country would be the following:

$$F_K^d = \beta r + (1 - \beta)\frac{\rho}{(1 - t^d)} \tag{2.21}$$

for the home country and

$$F_K^f = \beta r \frac{(1 - t^d)}{(1 - t^f)} + (1 - \beta)\frac{\rho}{(1 - t^f)} \tag{2.22}$$

for the foreign country, where ρ is the required rate of return on equity investment. Compared to a situation where the firm can only raise funds in the country where the real investment (K) takes place,[16] the foreign country now has a lower cost of capital. Moreover, the government of the home country loses tax revenue amounting to $t^d \beta K^f$ while the foreign country government gains $t^f \beta K^f$. The implications for the nationally optimal tax policy will be discussed further below.

2.6.2   Foreign Tax Credit Regimes

Consider now the case of a foreign tax credit regime. Normally, governments do not refund taxes when the host country tax liability is more than the home country tax liability. Under the foreign tax credit system, the government will levy tax on income earned in or repatriated from the foreign jurisdiction by a multinational reduced by a foreign tax credit for taxes paid to the host country. Under the *accrual* system, a tax is imposed on income earned abroad whether or not it is repatriated back to the home country. This treatment is commonly

---

[16] In this case, the cost of capital in the foreign country would be $F_K^f = \beta r + (1 - \beta)\frac{\rho}{(1 - t^f)}$.

used for the taxation of branch income and passive income earned by controlled-foreign corporations. Under the *deferral* system, income is only taxed if repatriated back to the home country. The tax will therefore be imposed on dividends but not on profits reinvested in foreign entities.

2.6.2.1   The Accrual System

In the case of accrual taxation, the domestic tax on foreign profits is equal to $t^d \left(F^f(K^f) - rB^f \right)$. The tax is reduced by a foreign tax credit equal to $t^f \left(F^f(K^f) - rB^f \right)$. As long as the foreign and home government define the multinational tax base as the same in both countries, the tax on income earned by the multinational in the foreign country is equal to $t^d \left(F^f(K^f) - rB^f \right)$ if $t^d \geq t^f$ (deficient tax credit position) and equal to $t^f \left(F^f(K^f) - rB^f \right)$ if $t^f \geq t^d$ (excess credit position). Thus, the tax rate on foreign source income is $\max(t^f, t^d)$ and the profits of the multinational firm are

$$P = (1 - t^d) \left(F^d(K^d) - rB^d \right) + (1 - \max(t^f, t^d)) \left(F^f(K^f) - rB^f \right).$$

(2.23)

As a consequence, if $t^d \geq t^f$, there are no gains from shifting debt from the foreign country to the home country. In this case, the costs of capital in the home country is given by

$$F_K^d = \beta r + (1 - \beta) \frac{\rho}{(1 - t^d)}.$$

(2.24a)

The cost of capital for investment in the foreign country is the same:

$$F_K^f = \beta r + (1 - \beta) \frac{\rho}{(1 - t^d)}.$$

(2.24b)

In contrast, if $t^f > t^d$, and given that there is accrual taxation, the foreign tax credit system is equivalent to the exemption system, i.e. the analysis of the preceding section applies.

2.6.2.2   The Deferral Tax System

The deferral tax system generally applies in the case that the multinational business is organized as a foreign subsidiary in the host country.

Dividends and other charges remitted to the parent are subject to tax by the home country. Assuming no withholding tax on dividends, the home country tax is equal to $t^d D/(1 - t^f)$ (D denoting dividends paid by the subsidiary to the parent). The foreign tax credit is equal to the corporate income taxes deemed to be paid on distributed profits $d\left(F^f(K^f) - rB^f\right)t^f$, d being the dividend payout ratio of the subsidiary. If the profit measured for tax purposes by the home country is the same as that taxed by host country, then the dividend payout ratio is simply the dividend D divided by after tax profits in the foreign country $d = D/\left[\left(F^f(K^f) - rB^f\right)(1 - t^f)\right]$. Therefore, the foreign tax credit is $t^f D/(1 - t^f)$. If $t^d \geq t^f$, the repatriation tax to the home country is thus equal to

$$t^d D/(1 - t^f) - t^f D/(1 - t^f) = \frac{(t^d - t^f)}{(1 - t^f)} D \equiv \Theta D. \qquad (2.25\text{a})$$

The multinational's income in the presence of the deferral system is equal to the following

$$P = (1 - t^d)\left(F^d(K^d) - rB^d\right) + (1 - t^f)\left(F^f(K^f) - rB^f\right) - \Theta D. \qquad (2.25\text{b})$$

It is clear, therefore, that the optimal financial strategy is for the subsidiary not to pay dividends to the parent in order to avoid the repatriation tax. With reinvestment of profits (therefore deferral of the home country tax), the cost of equity finance would be equal to the discount rate for equity finance.

The deferral method therefore results in a model somewhat similar to the pecking order model[17] in that reinvestment of profits is preferable to financing investment with new equity. As Hartmann [38] and Sinn [79] have pointed out, a firm in its gestation phase of growth may not have sufficient internal cash flow to finance investment. It must either rely on tax deductible debt or take equity

---

[17] The pecking order model introduced by Myers and Majluf [69] considers a situation where firm owners or managers are better informed about the profitability of their projects than outside investors. In this framework, the model shows that firms will prefer to finance their investment through retained earnings because financing via external equity would be a bad signal to the capital market.

transfers from the parent. If transfers of equity are used, the multinational anticipates that the income is "trapped" in the subsidiary in that any future dividends paid would attract the repatriation tax. Therefore, the cost of equity finance is greater for parent transfers compared to reinvested earnings. However, debt finance may still be more attractive to use than retained profits to finance the subsidiary's capital investments. Some countries try to limit deferral through limitations on the amount of reinvested profits that qualify for exempt taxation [84].

If the firm is in its mature stage, i.e. it needs no external financing, the cost of capital for the multinational for the deferral case would be the following:

$$F_K^d = \beta r + (1 - \beta) \frac{\rho}{(1 - t^d)} \qquad (2.26\text{a})$$

for the home country and

$$F_K^f = \beta r + (1 - \beta) \frac{\rho}{(1 - t^f)} \qquad (2.26\text{b})$$

for the foreign country.

Compared to the accrual method (equation (2.24b)), and given $t^f < t^d$, the cost of capital is lower in the foreign country since the subsidiary avoids payment of home country taxes on the income earned by the foreign subsidiary.

2.6.3   Some Complications

The above characterization of multinational finance in the presence of the foreign tax credit regime is typically used for analysis. However, it fails to account for some important tax planning complexities, depending on the existing regime.

One issue is that home countries may not define the income of the foreign subsidiary in the same way as the host country [58]. For example, the US and the UK use a different definition of income to determine the tax base of the subsidiary than that used by the host country. For example, suppose y^f is the taxable income of the subsidiary as defined by the foreign country tax authorities (for example, some income could be exempt or cost deductions differ from accounting cost measures). Suppose further that the home country defines taxable income of the subsidiary as y^d. In this case, the foreign tax credit is given by $dy^f t^f$ while the dividend pay out ratio is calculated as $d = D/\left(y^d(1 - t^f)\right)$, so that the repatriation tax would therefore be equal to $\frac{(t^d - t^f)}{(1 - t^f)} \frac{y^d}{y^f} D$. Since $y^d \neq y^f$, the repatriation tax is no longer exogenous – instead the ratio of y^d/y^f will depend on the capital stock and financing decisions of the subsidiary. Therefore, the cost of capital for the subsidiary should incorporate the impact of capital stock decisions on the repatriation tax. In some situations, the cost of capital could be lower if the capital stock decision expands taxable income of the host country so much more than that defined by the home country such that the repatriation tax declines. Further, it is no longer the case that it may be optimal to only reinvest profits – instead, it might be optimal to repatriate dividends especially if it permits greater use of debt finance that has its own tax benefits.

A further complication is that foreign tax credit systems often permit multinationals to calculate tax liabilities on income remitted from various sources on a "global basis." Income received from several sources (different countries or different types of income such as interest and dividends) are aggregated to calculate the home country's tax liability and foreign tax credits. Thus, excess tax credits on high-tax foreign sources of income (due to high foreign tax rates) can be used to offset the repatriation tax owing on income lightly taxed by foreign tax jurisdictions. Thus, multinationals when repatriating income earned from abroad average foreign tax rates to avoid paying the repatriation tax (see [2]). This can be achieved, for example, by simultaneously repatriating dividend and host country tax deductible charges paid by the subsidiary such as royalty income (the latter often subject to low withholding tax rates). They will also try to repatriate income with as little excess tax credits as possible – otherwise, they are paying too much tax to foreign income. Thus, a multinational firm in an excess tax credit position will push up leverage in foreign subsidiaries that are subject to high levels of tax.

2.6.4   Third Country Financing

A typical international tax planning strategy at the international level is to route financing through third countries rather than the parent transferring directly funds to finance subsidiary investments [63]. An example of this strategy is the following:

(1) The parent borrows to finance a transfer of equity to a subsidiary operating in a jurisdiction with a low tax regime (the tax preference provided is possibly limited to income earned by international financing entities). Usually, the jurisdiction chosen is one with a tax treaty with the home country.

(2) Little or no withholding taxes are imposed on dividends repatriated from the entity to the parent. The parent may be exempt from paying corporate tax on the dividends or may be in an excess credit position if the home country taxes foreign income with a credit on a global basis.

(3) The financing entity in the intermediary country lends funds to a subsidiary in the host country.

(4) The subsidiary remits interest, often exempt from withholding tax by treaty. Such interest earned by the financing entity is exempt from taxation by the home country since the interest is viewed as paid from active business income rather than passive income (passive income may be subject to accrual taxation by the home country).

(5) Effectively, the multinational is able to deduct interest incurred to finance a subsidiary in two jurisdictions – in the host country and home country.

Other structures similar to the above are used for insurance receipts, factoring and service charges. Many possible third country regimes are available to multinationals to take advantage of the tax benefits provided through intermediary financing. Depending on treaty arrangements, these include low-tax regimes in Barbados, Ireland, Belgium, Netherlands, Switzerland, Cyprus and Mauritius. The key elements are little or no withholding taxes imposed on dividends and other remitted income, low taxes imposed by the intermediary country and the absence or low taxes levied by the home country on income earned in the intermediary country. It is frequent to route income through many countries, creating multiple deductions for interest expense for one investment project.

These financing schemes lower the cost of capital. Effectively, for each dollar of borrowing by the subsidiary, interest expense is written off at the rate t^f in the host country and, in addition, at the rate t^d in the home country. Ignoring some small transaction and tax costs for routing income through the intermediary country, the effective cost of debt finance for investment in the host country is $r\left(1 - t^d - t^f\right)$. This implies that the cost of capital is the following:

$$F_K^d = \beta r + (1 - \beta)\frac{\rho}{(1 - t^d)} \tag{2.27a}$$

for the home country and

$$F_K^f = \beta r\frac{(1 - t^f - t^d)}{(1 - t^f)} + (1 - \beta)\frac{\rho}{(1 - t^f)} \tag{2.27b}$$

for the foreign country. Note that given that $r\left(1 - t^d - t^f\right)$ is less than $r(1 - t^f)$ foreign direct investment may be taxed at a negative effective tax rate.

2.6.5   Implications of Financial Arbitrage for Tax Competition

How will the possibility of financial arbitrage affect incentives for tax competition? A simple model of tax competition with financial arbitrage is developed in Mintz and Smart [62], and their main theoretical result may be derived as follows. Assume for simplicity that the governments of both the domestic and the foreign country pursue the objective to maximize corporate tax revenue, which we denote by T^d and T^f, respectively. Assume further that the level of debt for the firm as a whole must be zero, i.e. $B^d + B^f = 0$. This implies that debt financing can only occur in the form of a credit from the parent company to the subsidiary, financed by issuing equity in the domestic country or vice versa. We also assume that the level of debt in a jurisdiction cannot exceed the level of real investment (K). The optimal financing strategy of the firm is the following. Assume that the domestic country is the high tax country, i.e. $t^d > t^f$. In this case, the firm will simply issue equity $K^d + K^f$ in the foreign country and give a credit of K^d to the parent company. Effectively, domestic investment is thus entirely debt financed. The firm's overall profits are

$$P = (1 - t^d)\left(F^d(K^d) - rK^d\right) + (1 - t^f)\left(F^f(K^f) + rK^d\right). \quad (2.28)$$

What are the implications for tax revenue? Tax revenue in the domestic (high tax) country is

$$T^d = t^d\left(F^d(K^d) - rK^d\right). \quad (2.29)$$

For the foreign country, we have

$$T^f = t^f\left(F^f(K^f) + rK^d\right). \quad (2.30)$$

The key theoretical result derived by Mintz and Smart [62] is that there is no symmetric Nash equilibrium. Firstly, if $t^d = t^f > 0$, country $d(f)$ can achieve an increase of its tax base by $rK^f(rK^d)$ through a marginal reduction of its tax rate. Secondly, $t^d = t^f = 0$ cannot be an equilibrium because each country could raise its tax revenue by increasing its tax rate. As a result, there can only be an asymmetric equilibrium, where one country pursues a high tax strategy and the other country sets low taxes in order to attract tax part of the tax base from the high tax country.[18] A high tax country may be efficient if domestic investment earns high inframarginal rents. Levying high tax rates in order to tax these rents may make it worthwhile to tolerate some income shifting to other countries.

While Mintz and Smart [62] focus on the corporate income tax as an instrument to tax economic rents, Fuest and Hemmelgarn [23] consider a model where the corporate income tax serves as a backstop to

---

[18] Mintz and Smart [62] argue that the observed subfederal tax policy in Canada supports these findings. While all provinces have significant corporate income tax rates, one province, Quebec, imposes statutory tax rates which are significantly lower than those of other provinces.

the personal income tax. The private portfolio investment of households is subject to residence-based taxation. In their model, firms may use internal and external debt to shift income to a tax haven country. In the absence of income shifting, the optimal tax policy in this model implements production efficiency, i.e. the tax system distorts domestic savings but the tax on the marginal investment is zero. If the possibility of income shifting via debt is introduced, high tax countries respond by reducing their corporate tax rates. This gives rise to a subsidy on domestic real investment. In order to correct for this subsidy, it is optimal for the high tax countries to reduce depreciation allowances. The model thus explains tax rate cut cum base broadening policies as an attempt to limit income shifting without distorting domestic investment.

2.6.6   Conclusions: Tax Competition and Financial Arbitrage

Although there are some significant issues involved with modelling the cost of capital and finance for multinational investments, it is clear that there are a number of international tax planning issues that result in either higher or lower costs of capital for multinationals relative to companies only investing in domestic markets. Thus, depending on circumstances, taxes could either favour or discourage cross-border investments relative to domestic investments.

The possibility of shifting income from high to low tax jurisdictions through financing operations brings a new dimension to international tax competition. Although there is yet relatively little theoretical work on tax competition with financial arbitrage, the existing literature has shown that the emerging results differ significantly from those derived in traditional models of tax competition. In particular, there is a subtle interaction between financial arbitrage and the cost of capital for real investment which needs to be investigated further.

3

Tax Coordination

In the preceding section, we have discussed the tax policy countries pursue to maximize national welfare and the way in which they interact. It is clear from the analysis in the preceding sections that the interaction of the policies of individual countries does not necessarily lead to outcomes which are efficient for the economy as a whole. Many contributions to the literature therefore argue that countries should coordinate their tax policies. One key question in this debate is whether tax rates are too high or too low under tax competition. Another key issue in the literature on tax coordination is the question of whether tax competition may be a desirable limitation of the taxing powers of national governments due to political economy considerations. This section surveys the rapidly growing literature dealing with these issues.

3.1　Fiscal Externalities and the Welfare Effects of Tax Coordination

The welfare effects of tax coordination are usually analyzed by considering a coordinated marginal change in one tax instrument, holding constant the other tax instruments and departing from the equilibrium under tax competition. It is a common feature of all models discussed in Section 2 that the welfare of the representative citizen in the two countries can be expressed as a function of the two tax instruments, i.e. $W^j = W^j(t^d, t^f)$, $j = d, f$. In the absence of tax coordination, each country maximizes its objective function and takes as given the policy of the other country. The equilibrium is characterized by the first order conditions $W^j_{t^j} = 0$, $j = d, f$. In this framework, the welfare effect of a coordinated change in tax rates $dt^d = dt^f = dt$ is given by $dW^j = W^j_{t^j} dt^j + W^j_{t^i} dt^i$, $j = d, f$, $i = d, f$, $i \neq j$. Since $W^j_{t^j} = 0$, $j = d, f$, holds in the initial equilibrium, the welfare effect of the coordinated tax change is reduced to $dW^j = W^j_{t^i} dt^i$, $j = d, f$, $i = d, f$, $i \neq j$. The welfare effects of tax coordination thus depend on the way in which the welfare of individual countries is affected by the tax policies of other countries. These interaction effects are referred to as fiscal externalities. In general, fiscal externalities may be positive or negative. In the following, we provide an example where the fiscal externality of tax increases is positive, so that tax rates under tax competition are inefficiently low.

3.2   An Example: Tax Competition and the Underprovision of Public Goods

There is a large number of contributions arguing that tax competition will lead to levels of taxes and public expenditure that are below the optimal level for the economy as a whole [8, 86, 89, 93]. In this section, we reproduce the basic argument that leads to the underprovision result.

We consider a variant of the model used in Section 2.4. Assume that the world consists of two countries d and f which are linked by the direct investment of the multinational firm and a common market for portfolio capital, where households from both countries may invest their savings at the interest rate r. Assume further that the endowment of private households with capital is the same in both countries, i.e. $S^d = S^f$. Firms finance their investment via the international capital market. There is no residence-based taxation of income from savings, the income of the fixed factor accrues to the government and the multinational firm is taxed according to the exemption system. Under these assumptions, the profits of the multinational firm are

$$P = (1 - t^d)\left(F^d(K^d, L^d) - w^d L^d\right)$$

$$+ (1 - t^f)\left(F^f(K^f, L^f) - w^f L^f\right) - r(K^d + K^f). \tag{3.1}$$

The optimal levels of K^d and K^f are given by $(1 - t^d)F_K^d = r$ and $(1 - t^f)F_K^f = r$. Since there are only two countries, capital market equilibrium is given by the equation

$$S^d + S^f = K^d + K^f. \tag{3.2}$$

Equation (3.2) determines the interest rate r as a function of the two corporate tax rates, i.e. $r = r(t^d, t^f)$, with

$$r_{t^d} = -\frac{F_K^d F_{KK}^f(1 - t^f)}{F_{KK}^d(1 - t^d) + F_{KK}^f(1 - t^f)},$$

$$r_{t^f} = -\frac{F_K^f F_{KK}^d(1 - t^d)}{F_{KK}^d(1 - t^d) + F_{KK}^f(1 - t^f)}. \tag{3.3}$$

Note further that the capital demand functions can be written as $K^j = K^j(t^j, t^i)$, $j = d, f$, $i = d, f$, $i \neq j$, with

$$K_{t^j}^j = \frac{F_K^j}{F_{KK}^d(1 - t^d) + F_{KK}^f(1 - t^f)} < 0,$$

$$K_{t^i}^j = -\frac{F_K^i}{F_{KK}^d(1 - t^d) + F_{KK}^f(1 - t^f)} > 0. \tag{3.4}$$

The welfare of country j, $j = d, f$, is given by

$$W^j = M(C^j) + H(G^j) \tag{3.5}$$

where C^j is private consumption and G^j is the level of public goods provision. In equilibrium, after tax profits of the multinational firm will be zero $(P = 0)$.[1] Given that the income of the fixed factor accrues to

---

[1] This implies that the multinational's country of residence is irrelevant. Countries are effectively symmetric.

the government, we have $C^j = rS^j$ and $G^j = F^j(K^j, L^j) - rK^j$. The welfare function can be written as

$$W^j = M(rS^j) + H\left(F^j(K^j, L^j) - rK^j\right). \tag{3.6}$$

The optimal tax policy under tax competition maximizes (3.6) over t^j, which yields

$$W_{t^j}^j = (M_C S^j - H_G K^j)r_{t^j} + H_G\left(F_K^j(K^j, L^j) - r\right)K_{t^j}^j = 0. \tag{3.7}$$

This can be rearranged to

$$W_{t^j}^j = (M_C S^j - H_G K^j)r_{t^j} + H_G t^j F_K^j(K^j, L^j)K_{t^j}^j = 0. \tag{3.8}$$

In a symmetric equilibrium with $t^d = t^f$, our assumption $S^d = S^f$ implies $K^j = S^j$, $j = d, f$. The equilibrium tax rates are given by

$$t^{j*} = \frac{(H_G - M_C)K^j}{H_G F_K^j}\frac{r_{t^j}}{K_{t^j}^j} \quad j = d, f. \tag{3.9}$$

The equilibrium under tax competition will thus be characterized by positive corporate tax rates if $H_G - M_C > 0$. This condition holds if, at $t^d = t^f = 0$, revenue from the fixed factor is insufficient to finance a first best level of public goods provision (where $H_G = M_C$). In this case, a positive tax has the benefit of reducing the interest rate, which shifts income from the private to the public sector.[2] The cost of the tax is that it distorts investment.

What are the welfare effects of tax coordination in this framework? Assume that both countries coordinate their tax policies and jointly change their corporate tax rates by dt, departing from the equilibrium without coordination. The additional tax revenue is used to increase G^j. As demonstrated in the preceding section, the effect on the welfare of country j can be written as $dW^j = W_{t^i}^j dt^i$. This implies

$$dW^j/dt = W_{t^i}^j = (M_C - H_G)K^j r_{t^i} + H_G\left(F_K^j(K^j, L^j) - r\right)K_{t^i}^j. \tag{3.10}$$

---

[2] Hoyt [46] analyzes a model of tax competition with source-based capital taxes and shows that the tax rate is smaller, the higher the number of countries competing for capital. This reflects that the decline in the interest rate caused by a tax increase in one country is smaller, the smaller this country is, relative to the world economy.

The right-hand side of (3.10) allows to identify the fiscal externalities which determine the welfare effects of tax coordination. The first term on the right-hand side of (3.10) reflects that an increase of the tax rate in country i reduces the interest rate r. The decline in the interest rate shifts resources from the private sector to the public sector. Since $H_G - M_C > 0$ in the initial equilibrium, this increases welfare. The second term reflects that a tax increase in country i induces a capital flow from country i to country j. Country j benefits from this capital inflow if the marginal productivity of capital exceeds the interest rate. This is the case if investment is distorted, i.e. if $t^j > 0$. Thus, a coordinated capital tax increase, where the additional tax revenue is used to provide more public goods, unambiguously increases welfare. A large part of the literature on tax coordination takes this result as a point of reference.

Equation (3.10) also shows that the welfare effect of tax coordination is zero if the revenue the government collects from the fixed factor is sufficient to provide the optimal quantity of G, so that $H_G = M_C$. In this case, (3.9) shows that both countries would set $t^j = 0$ and the right-hand side of (3.10) would be zero. Thus, if the marginal source of government revenue is a nondistortionary tax, no need for tax coordination arises.[3]

Many contributions to the literature on tax coordination use models where countries are assumed to be small, i.e. governments neglect the effect of their tax policy on the interest rate. In our model, this would imply that $r_{t^j} = 0$, $j = d, f$. In this case, tax competition would lead to the result $t^d = t^f = 0$. In this case, the welfare effect of a coordinated increase in taxes by dt is given by $dW^j/dt = (M_C - H_G)K^j(dr/dt)$. Since the supply of capital to the economy as a whole is fixed, the change in the interest rate is simply $dr/dt = -F_K^j$. Again, the coordinated tax increase increases public sector revenue by reducing the interest rate r. If $H_G - M_C > 0$ in the initial equilibrium, this increases welfare.

---

[3] The role of tax distortions for the phenomenon of fiscal externalities is emphasized by Bucovetsky and Wilson [8]. The finding that there are no benefits from tax coordination if public expenditure is financed by nondistortionary taxes, at the margin, can be found in Oates and Schwab [71].

3.3   Residence-Based Capital Income Taxation

A limitation of the analysis in the preceding sections is that residence-based taxes on the portfolio income of households were ruled out. As pointed out in Section 2.4, this assumption may be justified by the fact that it is relatively easy for taxpayers to avoid residence-based taxes. In the debate on tax coordination, though, residence-based capital income taxation plays an important role. More cooperation in the enforcement of these taxes is a goal of tax coordination of its own. A key argument in favour of cooperation in enforcing residence-based capital income taxation is that the availability of residence-based taxes reduces the need for other forms of tax coordination. Bucovetsky and Wilson [8] consider a model where the available tax instruments are a source tax and a residence-based tax on capital. In this case, tax policy under tax competition is efficient and nothing can be gained from tax coordination,

The important role of residence-based taxes can be demonstrated using a slightly extended version of the model developed above. Assume that, next to the corporate income tax t, which is effectively a source-based capital tax, the government of country j, $j = d, f$, may raise a residence-based tax on the household's income from savings. In this case, the household's income from savings will be a function of the after tax return on savings which we denote by r^{nj}. The residence-based tax collected per unit of savings is given by $r - r^{nj}$.

In the preceding sections, we have assumed that savings are fixed. This assumption makes sense as long as income from savings is untaxed. But if residence-based capital income taxes are available, the assumption of fixed savings implies that the savings tax is effectively a lump sum tax. This neglects that residence-based capital income taxes distort the savings decision. We therefore extend the model used in the preceding section as follows. Households live for two periods. In the first period, they receive and endowment E which is identical for both countries and which may be used for savings S^j or consumption in period 1, denoted by C_1^j. The first period budget constraint is thus $C_1^j = E - S^j$. Utility from private consumption is given by $M = M(C_1^j, C_2^j)$, where C_2^j is private consumption in period 2. The private sector budget constraint in period 2 is $C_2^j = (1 + r^{nj})S^j$, where r^{nj} is after tax rate of return on portfolio investment received by a household residing in country j. The availability of residence-based taxes on savings implies that r^{nj} can be controlled by the government. Maximizing $M = M(C_1^j, C_2^j)$ subject to the two budget constraints yields a savings function $S^j = S^j(r^{nj})$. For the following analysis, we assume that the savings function has a positive slope, i.e. $S_{r^{nj}}^j > 0$. It is straightforward to derive the indirect utility function $V^j = V^j(r^{nj})$, with $V_{r^{nj}}^j = M_{C_2^j}S^j$.

The multinational firm invests in period 1 and produces its output in period 2. Profits of the multinational firm, which accrue in period 2, are given by

$$P = (1 - t^d)\left(F^d(K^d, L^d) - w^d L^d\right)$$

$$+ (1 - t^f)\left(F^f(K^f, L^f) - w^f L^f\right) - r(K^d + K^f). \tag{3.11}$$

The optimal levels of K^d and K^f are given by $(1 - t^d)F_K^d = r$ and $(1 - t^f)F_K^f = r$. The capital market equilibrium is given by the equation

$$S^d(r^{nd}) + S^f(r^{nf}) = K^d + K^f. \tag{3.12}$$

Equation (3.12) determines the interest rate r as a function of the two corporate tax rates and the two after tax rates of return on savings, i.e. $r = r(t^d, t^f, r^{nd}, r^{nf})$, with

$$r_{t^d} = -\frac{F_K^d F_{KK}^f(1 - t^f)}{F_{KK}^d(1 - t^d) + F_{KK}^f(1 - t^f)} < 0,$$

$$r_{t^f} = -\frac{F_K^f F_{KK}^d(1 - t^d)}{F_{KK}^d(1 - t^d) + F_{KK}^f(1 - t^f)} < 0 \tag{3.13}$$

and

$$r_{r^{nd}} = S_{r^{nd}}\frac{F_{KK}^d F_{KK}^f(1 - t^f)(1 - t^d)}{F_{KK}^d(1 - t^d) + F_{KK}^f(1 - t^f)} < 0,$$

$$r_{r^{nf}} = S_{r^{nd}}\frac{F_{KK}^f F_{KK}^d(1 - t^d)(1 - t^f)}{F_{KK}^d(1 - t^d) + F_{KK}^f(1 - t^f)} < 0. \tag{3.14}$$

Given this, the capital demand functions can be written as $K^j = K^j(t^j, t^i, r^{nj}, r^{ni})$, $j = d, f$, $i = d, f$, $i \neq j$, with

$$K^j_{t^j} = \frac{F^j_K}{F^d_{KK}(1 - t^d) + F^f_{KK}(1 - t^f)} < 0,$$

$$K^j_{t^i} = -\frac{F^i_K}{F^d_{KK}(1 - t^d) + F^f_{KK}(1 - t^f)} > 0 \tag{3.15}$$

and

$$K^j_{r^{nj}} = S_{r^{nj}} \frac{F^i_{KK}(1 - t^i)}{F^d_{KK}(1 - t^d) + F^f_{KK}(1 - t^f)} < 0,$$

$$K^j_{r^{ni}} = S_{r^{ni}} \frac{F^i_{KK}(1 - t^i)}{F^d_{KK}(1 - t^d) + F^f_{KK}(1 - t^f)} < 0. \tag{3.16}$$

Public consumption takes place only in period 2. The public sector budget constraint is

$$G^j = (r - r^{nj})S^j + F^j(K^j, L^j) - rK^j. \tag{3.17}$$

The welfare of the representative citizen can be written as

$$W^j = V^j(r^{nj}) + H\left((r - r^{nj})S^j + F^j(K^j, L^j) - rK^j\right). \tag{3.18}$$

Governments maximize (3.18) over t^j and r^{nj}. The first-order conditions for t^j and r^{nj} are given by

$$W^j_{t^j} = H_G\left(F^j_K(K^j, L^j) - r\right)K^j_{t^j} + H_G(S^j - K^j)r_{t^j} = 0 \tag{3.19}$$

and

$$W^j_{r^{nj}} = (M_{C_2} - H_G)S^j + H_G(r - r^{nj})S^j_{r^{nj}}$$

$$+ H_G\left(F^j_K(K^j, L^j) - r\right)K^j_{r^{nj}} + H_G(S^j - K^j)r_{r^{nj}} = 0. \tag{3.20}$$

Using $F^j_K - r = t^j F^j_K$ and given that symmetry implies $S^j = K^j$, (3.19) yields $t^j = 0$ and (3.20) can be rearranged to

$$r - r^{nj} = \frac{(H_G - M_{C_2})}{H_G} \frac{S^j}{S^j_{r^{nj}}}. \tag{3.21}$$

The right-hand side of (3.21) is positive if $H_G - M_{C_2} > 0$, i.e. if, at $r - r^{nj} = 0$ and $t^j = 0$, revenue from the fixed factor is insufficient to finance the optimal level of the public consumption good. In this case (3.19) and (3.20) imply that a symmetric equilibrium emerges with zero corporate tax rates ($t^j = 0$, $j = d, f$) and positive residence-based capital income tax rates ($r - r^{nj} > 0$). The optimal tax policy distorts savings, rather than domestic investment.

What are the effects of tax coordination in this framework? As in the preceding section, we consider a marginal increase in the corporate income tax rates, departing from the equilibrium under tax competition. The additional revenue raised is spent on public consumption and r^{nj} is held constant. The welfare effect is given by

$$dW^j/dt = W^j_{t^i} = H_G \left(F^j_K(K^j, L^j) - r \right) K^j_{t^i} + H_G(S^j - K^j)r_{t^i}.$$

(3.22)

In the initial equilibrium, $t^j = 0$ so that $F^j_K(K^j, L^j) - r = 0$. Moreover, symmetry implies $S^j = K^j$, so that the right-hand side of (3.22) is equal to zero. The coordinated tax change neither increases nor reduces welfare. Bucovetsky and Wilson [8] explain the absence of gains from tax coordination in the presence of both source and residence-based capital taxes in their model[4] as follows: "The presence of both taxes allows a government to manipulate gross and net returns to capital... independently of the world return... With both taxes, the region is effectively able to insulate itself from the capital flows that occur in response to another region's tax and expenditure policy." [8, p. 349]. It thus turns out that the availability of tax instruments is crucial for the question of whether or not public goods are underprovided under tax competition.[5]

3.4 Distortionary Labour Taxes

Another contribution made by Bucovetsky and Wilson [8] is to analyse the effects of tax coordination under the assumption that, next to

---

[4] The main differences to the model considered here is that Bucovetsky and Wilson [8] consider small open economies, where governments take the interest rate as given.

[5] Tax coordination with multiple tax instruments is further analysed in Eggert and Genser [15].

source-based capital taxes, governments may also levy a tax on labor income. Since labor supply is endogenous, this tax is also distortionary. It turns out that, under tax competition, the capital tax is zero and public expenditure is financed exclusively by the labor tax, although this tax distorts the labor-leisure choice of the representative household. The reason for this result is that, since the supply of capital is perceived as infinitely elastic by each individual country, the burden of a capital tax would be borne by the factor labor anyway. It is more efficient to tax this factor directly.

The analysis in Bucovetsky and Wilson [8] also leads to the conclusion that there is an underprovision of public goods under tax competition. Both the source-based capital tax and the labor tax are inefficiently low. The reason for the undertaxation of wages is that an increase in the wage tax rate to finance more public expenditure triggers a positive fiscal externality. The higher wage tax rate reduces labor supply and thus reduces the marginal productivity of capital in the country under consideration. This triggers a capital flow to other countries. These countries benefit from the capital inflow although capital is not taxed because the capital inflow raises the marginal productivity of labor and, hence, labor supply. It is now the wage tax that drives a wedge between the marginal social cost of labor, which equals the net wage, and the marginal benefit, that is the gross wage.

3.5   Tax Competition and Optimal Redistributive Income Taxation

A further extension of available tax instruments, along with a relaxation of the assumption of perfect information and identical households, is considered by Huber [47], who analyses tax competition in a Mirrlees–Stiglitz type model of optimum income taxation. In each country, there are two types of individuals which differ with respect to their earning abilities and have different endowments with capital. Capital taxation according to the residence principle is ruled out. The government uses a non-linear income tax system to finance a public good and redistribute income between individuals. Redistributive policies are constrained by the fact that abilities cannot be observed directly. The government therefore faces an incentive compatibility constraint. In this framework, the result that capital taxes tend to be too low under tax competition is confirmed for the case where individuals with higher abilities also own more capital than low ability individuals. Essentially, a capital tax increase in all jurisdictions would then redistribute income from high to low ability individuals. This leads to a welfare gain, given the second-best nature of redistributive policies in this model. This result implies that the potential gains from tax coordination may increase if the distribution of wealth becomes more unequal and vice versa.

Fuest and Huber [25] also consider tax competition and tax coordination in a model where tax policy aims at redistributing income and faces informational constraints. In their model, individuals have equal abilities but differ with respect to their endowment with capital. Governments are able to levy a residence-based capital income tax and tax labour and capital income differently, but individuals may, at some cost, shift labour to capital income and vice versa to avoid taxes. The government can only observe reported income, that is labour and capital income after shifting has taken place. Since rich households may shift capital to labour income in order to mimick poor households, redistributive taxation has to take into account an incentive compatibility constraint. The optimal tax structure implies that, for poor households, the marginal tax rate on capital income is higher than the tax rate on labor income. This reduces the incentives for rich households to mimick poor households. In this framework, the authors consider a coordinated increase in the source-based capital tax. The additional revenue is used to compensate the two household types for the loss in capital income. Given this, the redistributive transfers are readjusted, so that the incentive compatibility constraint binds again.

This tax coordination agreement increases welfare because it relaxes the incentive compatibility constraint. The decline in interest rates caused by the coordinated tax increase reduces the incentives for mimicking because the compensation for the decline in interest rates received by mimickers is tailored to the capital endowment of poor households. The capital endowment of mimickers, however, is much larger. The reduced incentives for mimicking create additional room for income redistribution.

3.6 May Capital Taxes be Too High Under Tax Competition?

The literature discussed so far suggests that tax competition leads to an underprovision of public goods or to too little income redistribution, so that coordinated tax increases are desirable. However, there are several reasons why capital taxes may in fact be too high under tax competition. Moreover, coordinated capital tax increases may benefit only some countries while others lose. These issues are discussed in the following paragraphs.

3.6.1 Asymmetric Countries

In the contributions discussed so far, it has been assumed that tax coordination occurs among symmetric jurisdictions. De Pater and Myers [10] analyse a model where jurisdictions differ with respect to their endowments with capital. In this framework, capital taxes are used to strategically influence the interest rate in the international capital market. Capital importing countries tax domestic investment in order to reduce the interest rate whereas capital exporting countries do the opposite. It is clear that this leads to tax structures that are inefficient from the point of view of the economy as a whole, even if the governments may in principle use lump sum taxes to finance their expenditure. The reason is that the effect of tax policy on the interest rate gives rise to fiscal externalities. For instance, governments of capital exporting countries do not take into account that an increase in interest rates caused by a subsidy on domestic investment hurts capital importing countries. Therefore, capital taxes will be inefficiently high in capital importing regions and vice versa. In this case, welfare enhancing tax coordination should aim at reducing tax rate differences, i.e. capital exporting countries should increase their tax rates and capital importing countries should do the opposite.

While the idea that large countries may use their market power to strategically influence prices is familiar from international trade theory, asymmetries between countries also affect the working of tax competition in a more subtle way. Wilson [90] considers a two country model where the two jurisdictions are identical except for the size of the labour force.[6] He shows that, under tax competition, individuals are better off in the small country. The reason is that the capital tax raised by a country is higher, the stronger the effect of its capital demand on the interest rate in the international capital market, i.e. the lower the elasticity of capital supply. The capital demand of the large country has a stronger impact on the interest rate than that of the small country. The former therefore sets a higher capital tax rate. Since the cost of capital is thus lower in the small country, per capita investment is higher and, hence, the wage rate is also higher. This advantage of being small implies that, if the size difference is sufficiently large, the small country may actually be better off under tax competition, where public expenditure is financed, on the margin, with capital taxes[7], than in a coordinated equilibrium or a first-best situation where unrestricted lump sum taxes are available.[8]

The result that small countries benefit from tax competition, however, may not hold for all types of investment. Haufler and Wooton [41] argue that, in the presence of imperfect competition and transport costs, large countries may actually be at an advantage when countries compete for foreign direct investment. The model considered by these authors assumes that there is a multinational firm that sells its output in a goods market with imperfect competition. Since there are transport costs, the firm will prefer to locate in the larger market. This gives rise to a locational rent for the large country, which may be exploited by tax policy, which means that the large country may levy higher taxes (or offer lower subsidies) than the small country and will still receive the investment.

---

[6] Bucovetsky [7] analyses a similar model but restricts the analysis to quadratic production functions.

[7] These results also go through if a distortionary wage tax is available next to the capital tax. However, if the supply of public goods is endogenous (as opposed to a fixed revenue constraint), the gains of small countries from tax competition are reduced, see Eggert and Haufler [17] and Haufler [39], chapter 5.

[8] As Wilson [90] emphasizes, the result that small countries tend to benefit from tax competition is opposed to the findings of international trade theory and the theory of "tariff wars," where small countries are at a disadvantage (see [53]).

3.6.2   Tax Exportation and Foreign Firm Ownership

One important reason why tax competition may lead to over-rather than undertaxation is the phenomenon of tax exportation. Tax exportation occurs if governments raise taxes which are at least partly borne by the citizens of other jurisdictions. Richter and Wellisch [76] analyse a model with household and firm mobility and show, among other things, that foreign ownership of land gives rise to inefficiently high taxes on firms. Huizinga and Nielsen [48] consider a model where domestic firms are owned by foreigners and the taxation of pure profits is assumed to be restricted for exogenous reasons. In this framework, it turns out that countries will raise source taxes on capital in order to indirectly tax profits and thus shift income from foreign firm owners to domestic residents. It may even be optimal for an individual country to raise capital taxes and use the revenue to make lump sum payments to its citizens. In a world with an endogenous savings decision, this may give rise to an overtaxation of capital. Here, the nature of the emerging fiscal externality is quite obvious. Countries do not take into account that their capital taxes reduce the profit income and distort the savings decisions of households residing in other jurisdictions.[9]

Another form of tax exportation may occur in the presence of multinational firms. This issue is studied in Mintz and Tulkens [66]. They show that, under tax competition, corporate income taxation of individual countries gives rise to negative externalities. Two channels of these negative externalities are identified. Firstly, countries tax the profits of foreign multinationals operating within their borders, which reduces profit income accruing to other countries.[10] Secondly, countries tax the foreign profits of domestic multinational firms. This has a negative impact on foreign investment and therefore reduces the tax revenue and the income of immobile factors generated abroad. These negative fiscal externalities suggest that, in the presence of international

---

[9] Foreign firm ownership, though, may also give rise to suboptimally low corporate income taxes as shown by Fuest and Hemmelgarn [23], who consider a model where the corproate income tax serves as a backstop to the personal income tax.

[10] This negative externality is also at the heart of the analysis in Huizinga and Nielsen [48].

direct investment, tax competition may actually lead to over-rather than undertaxation of capital income.

Fuest and Huber [27] explicitly analyse the welfare effects of coordinated tax increases in the presence of multinational firms. They compare the effects of tax competition under the exemption system, the deduction system and the foreign tax credit system. The difference to Mintz and Tulkens [66] and Huizinga and Nielsen [48] is that no pure profits which would accrue to foreigners exist. It turns out that capital taxes may be too high under tax competition if countries apply the deduction system or the tax credit system while taxes are too low under the exemption system. The reason is that, under the exemption system, capital taxes are effectively purely source-based and rents are fully taxed, so that no tax exportation occurs. Under the deduction system and the tax credit system, domestic taxes partly fall on investment abroad and reduce the income of foreigners.

A different form of inefficiency caused by tax exportation is analysed by Wildasin and Wilson [88]. They consider a model where households would like to invest abroad in order to diversify risks. But the governments of individual jurisdictions have an incentive to levy confiscatory taxes on all assets owned by foreigners. This prevents risk diversification and reduces overall welfare.

The incentive to increase taxes if foreign firms are present raises the question whether foreign firm ownership may act as a break on tax rate reductions which are usually seen as a consequence of increasing economic integration. One limitation of the literature dealing with the implications of foreign firm ownership for tax competition and tax coordination is that the presence of foreign firms is taken as given. This is not satisfactory because the extent of foreign firm ownership will not be independent of the degree of economic integration and the level of taxes.[11] Fuest [22] considers a model where the number of foreign firms operating in a country is endogenous and depends on the tax policy pursued by the country and the degree of economic integration. Changes in the degree of economic integration are modeled as changes

---

[11] Kind et al. [55] show that, due to the presence of foreign owned firms, taxes may increase if economic integration proceeds. In their model, foreign firm ownership is also exogenous.

in trade costs and changes in tariffs. The analysis shows that increasing economic integration may be compatible with declining taxes and an increasing presence of foreign owned firms. Therefore, foreign firm ownership may not prevent corporate taxes from falling as economic integration proceeds.

3.6.3   Imperfect Competition in Labor Markets

Most of the literature of tax competition assumes that markets are perfectly competitive. This assumption is probably most problematic for labour markets. Especially in Europe, labour markets tend to be characterized by minimum wages and collective wage bargaining. Lejour and Verbon [60] consider a two country model with imperfect capital mobility, where wages are set by monopoly unions. The population in each country consists of workers, who may be employed or unemployed, and capital owners who may invest at home or abroad. The government runs a social insurance system consisting of a proportional wage tax that finances transfers to the unemployed. The strategic policy variable is the tax rate of the social insurance system. Increases in the tax rate are partly shifted to capital owners via higher wages. Capital owners will therefore prefer a lower tax rate than workers. The government is assumed to maximize a generalised utilitarian welfare function of all residents.

In this model, changes in the policy of an individual country also affects the welfare of other countries. However, the fiscal externality will affect foreign workers and foreign capital owners in different ways. Foreign workers will benefit from an increase in the domestic social insurance tax rate since it triggers a capital flow to the foreign country. Foreign capital owners, in contrast, are affected negatively because their investment opportunities are deteriorated. On balance, however, it turns out that the positive fiscal externality dominates such that, in terms of overall welfare, social security tax rates are too low under tax competition.

Fuest and Huber [24] also consider a model with a non-competitive labour market and unemployment. Countries are small, and the wage rate is determined via bargaining between unions and firms. The government in each country raises a wage tax and a source tax on capital to finance a public good. Under tax competition, the structure of wage and capital taxes is in general undetermined, which means that the equilibrium tax structure may differ from that emerging under competitive labour markets. The reason is that taxation may affect the outcome of wage bargaining. In this framework, it also turns out that the tax policy of individual countries gives rise to both positive and negative fiscal externalities. The positive externalities are similar to those found in models with competitive labour markets. The negative externalities are caused by the impact of capital flows on wage bargaining. A capital inflow may encourage unions to raise the wage rate in the bargaining process and thus worsen the labour market distortion. It turns out that the negative fiscal externality may dominate in this model, such that labour and capital tax rates are inefficiently high under tax competition.[12]

3.6.4 Political Economy Models

The theories of tax competition discussed so far are based on the assumption that governments maximize the welfare of their citizens. This implies that the analysis abstracts from inefficiencies caused by imperfections of the political process. Public choice theorists have argued that these imperfections of the political process give rise to excessive government growth. From this persepective, tax competition may be seen as a desirable check on the expansion of the public sector. The most radical version of this argument is due to Brennan and Buchanan [5], who model government as a revenue maximizing Leviathan without any interest in the well being of the citizens. If this view of government is taken seriously, it is clear that tax competition is a highly welcome way of restricting the power to tax. Obviously, a serious limitation of the Leviathan model is that it abstracts completely from institutions such as elections by which modern democracies

---

[12] Further contributions to issue of how tax competion affects tax policy in the presence of unemployment, but without reference to tax coordination, include Richter and Schneider [75], Eggert and Görke [16] and Leite-Monteiro, Marchand and Pestieau [59].

create incentives for the members of governments to take into account the welfare of citizens and voters.[13]

A somewhat more balanced approach is used by Edwards and Keen [14]. These authors consider a model of a large number of small open economies with capital mobility, where the stock of capital for the economy as a whole is fixed. It is assumed that governments maximize an objective function of the type $Z = Z(U, R)$, with $Z_U(U, R) \geq 0$ and $Z_R(U, R) \geq 0$, where U is the utility of the representative citizen and R is a variable that stands for resources wasted due to imperfections of the political process. The objective function Z may be interpreted as a voter support function and comprises the polar cases of a purely benevolent government $Z_R(U, R) = 0$ and that of a revenue maximizer $Z_U(U, R) = 0$.

The equilibrium under tax competition is characterized by a tax structure which is the same as that which would be chosen by a benevolent government, given the level of public expenditure. The reason is that politicians, whether selfish or benevolent, have no interest in raising revenue in an inefficient way. However, political economy considerations do make a difference with respect to the overall level and the structure of public expenditure; the structure is different because part of the revenue is now devoted to socially wasteful expenditure. In this setup, fiscal competition tends to limit government waste but also reduces socially desirable public expenditure. The authors show that a coordinated increase in capital taxes has an ambiguous effect on the welfare of the representative citizen. Welfare is more likely to increase, the higher the marginal excess burden of the tax system under tax competition and the lower the marginal propensity of the government to waste resources.[14]

---

[13] Frey and Eichenberger [20] emphasize that both economic distortions such as the underprovision of public goods and political distortions caused by imperfections of the political process should be taken into account in the analysis of tax competition.

[14] Fuest [21] extends the Edwards-Keen model by introducing a bureaucracy into the model. Politicians and bureaucrats have diverging interests and the political decision making process is modelled as a bargaining game between these two groups. It turns out that coordinated capital tax increases unambiguously reduce the welfare of the representative citizen if the bureaucrats dominate the decision making process. Sato [77] extends the Edwards-Keen model by explicitly considering a rent seeking game. The welfare effects of coordinated tax increases are also ambiguous.

Another set of political economy approaches to tax competition discusses the impact of increasing capital mobility on fiscal policy decisions. Persson and Tabellini [73] consider a two-stage variant of the median voter model where, in each country, a government is elected at stage one. The governments then set tax policy in a tax competition game played at stage two. In this model, the level of public expenditure is also given, such that the relevant decision is on the distribution of the tax burden between labour and capital. Increasing capital mobility has two opposing effects. On the one hand, there is what the authors call the "economic effect": greater capital mobility increases tax competition and therefore drives down the capital tax rate. On the other hand, the authors find a "political effect": Voters anticipate the behaviour of their governments in the tax competition game and will elect more "leftist" governments in order to prevent an excessive reduction of the capital tax rate.[15] On balance, however, the economic effect dominates and a larger part of the tax burden is borne by labour as capital mobility increases.

Fuest and Huber [26] analyse tax competition and tax coordination in a model where individuals differ with respect to their labour income and their capital endowments and fiscal policy decisions are taken via majority voting. The government in each country raises a labour income tax and a source-based capital tax and provides a local public good. Although the policy space is two-dimensional, a median voter equilibrium exists. The reason is that all voters, irrespective of their labour income, will prefer not to tax capital at source. For the wage tax and, hence, the level of expenditure on the local public good, the median voter's preferences will determine the policy outcome. In the equilibrium, the level of public good provision is determined by two countervailing forces. First, the level of public goods provision will be lower, the higher the marginal excess burden of the wage tax because

---

[15] An interesting variant of the approached developed in Persson and Tabellini [73] is analysed by Brückner [6]. He shows that, if voters anticipate that governments will coordinate taxes, tax competition may occur at the voting (or delegation) stage, i.e. voters will delegate politicians with low preferences for public goods. It is therefore unclear whether capital tax rates are higher under tax coordination compared to a regime of tax competition.

the median voter will also have to bear the cost of tax distortions. Second, the level of public goods provision will be higher, the greater the difference between average and median labour income. This reflects the redistributive nature of the local public good. All residents benefit equally from the provision of this good, but the median voter's share in the cost of the public good is proportional to labour income. In the empirically revelevant case where the median voter's income is below average income, there may thus be an overpovision of public goods under tax competition.

Grazzini and Ypersele [36] also consider problems of tax competition in a median voter model. The framework used is a two-country model with capital mobility, where the governments raise source taxes on capital and labour taxes. It is assumed, however, that the level of public expenditure is fixed, such that the voting decision is only over the mix between capital and labour taxes that finances the public budget. The authors show that, if countries are asymmetric, tax coordination agreements may fail to receive political support.

Gabszewicz and Ypersele [28] also consider the effects of increasing capital mobility in a political economy model where the strategic policy variable is a transfer to unemployed workers which also constitutes a minimum wage rate. The level of the minimum wage is determined via majority voting. Essentially, the voting outcome is determined by the factor endowment of the median voter. The minimum wage rate raises the income of employed workers but also reduces employment. It turns out that, even if the median voter is endowed with labour only, increasing capital mobility drives down the equilibrium minimum wage.

In a recent paper, Besley and Smart [3] analyse the role of fiscal restraints, which may be caused by fiscal competition, in a principal agent model of the political process with moral hazard and adverse selection. In this model, the quality of public policy depends on the extent to which restraining bad governments can be combined with an improved selection of politicians. The analysis shows that increasing fiscal restraints due to tax competition do not necessarily increase the welfare of voters. Paradoxically, it turns out that fiscal restraints may only be in the interest of voters if the share of benevolent politicians is high.

Taken together, political economy models of tax competition suggest two conclusions. Firstly, although imperfections of the political process are not sufficient to overturn the result that tax competition leads to inefficiently low tax rates, contributions neglecting political economy problems give rise to an excessively pessimistic assessment of the welfare implications of tax competition. Secondly, the literature dealing with the effects of increasing capital mobility on the distribution of the tax burden between capital and immobile labour seems to confirm the intuitively plausible view according to which higher capital mobility will induce tax policy changes in favor of capital owners.

3.7 Regional Versus Global Coordination

It has been assumed so far that tax coordination involves all countries in the world. But real world tax coordination initiatives are usually restricted to a certain subgroup of countries like the EU member states or the OECD countries. If capital tax coordination only takes place among a subset of countries, the problem arises that capital may still flow to countries not participating in the coordination agreements. This raises the question whether the arguments in favour of coordinated capital tax increases are still valid if there are third countries not participating in the coordination agreement. The answer is that, if the group of countries which participates in the coordination agreement is large enough to have an impact on the international interest rate, there are potential welfare gains from regional tax coordination (see also [56]). Sorensen [81, 82] analyses the welfare effects of regional tax coordination in simulation models and confirms the finding that there are welfare gains from regional tax coordination but also shows that these gains are lower than the gains from worldwide coordination.

Haufler and Wooton [42] focus on regional tax coordination in a model where countries compete for direct investment of an internationally mobile firm. They consider a world of three countries. Two of them may form a union and coordinate taxes. It turns out that there are two types of gains from regional tax coordination. Firstly, if the investment would be located in the union under tax competition, tax coordination within the union allows the country where the investment is located to extract higher rents from the firm. Secondly, tax coordination yields a benefit by internalizing fiscal externalities within the union. Interestingly, it is unclear whether regional tax coordination increases or decreases tax rates in this model.

4

Conclusions

The interaction of corporate income taxes and international capital flows suggests that the source-based capital taxes potentially result in quite significant distortions in the allocation of capital at the international level. Much economic analysis has viewed that capital taxes will disappear if real capital is perfectly mobile at the international level. However, given that this view assumes that economies are small and there are no impediments to the free flow of capital, reality would suggest that competition for real capital is less extreme than what typical economic models would suggest. There are good reasons for countries to tax mobile capital if governments can "export" taxes paid by non-residents. Competitiveness may make it more difficult for countries to tax income earned by foreigners but there is virtually no economic study that would suggest that real capital is perfectly mobile.[1]

Instead, the problems with corporate taxation are much deeper than what would be suggested by models with perfect mobility of real capital. One issue is that taxable profits are highly mobile, leading to the "tax base flight" fiscal externality dominating other fiscal externalities

---

[1] Of course, limited capital mobility does not necessarily imply that capital taxes survive, as is shown by Gordon and Bovenberg [34].

in this case. Governments have been trying to protect their tax bases by imposing restrictions that lead to an erosion of profits as well as reducing statutory tax rates. The other issue is that it is increasingly difficult to impose a tax on income earned in a jurisdiction by a growing multi-national sector in a more integrated global economy. New technology and financial transactions makes it more problematical to define profits earned in one country alone. Governments have been increasing their reliance on profit-based measures of transfer prices since these can rely more on allocation methods for global profits of multinationals rather than transaction-based rules. Nonetheless, administrative practices will require considerable co-operation amongst governments if they are to maintain the corporate income tax. Alternatively, governments might need to look for alternative taxes on businesses.

References

[1] R. Altshuler and H. Grubert, "Repatriation taxes, repatriation strategies and multinational financial policy," *Journal of Public Economics*, vol. 87, pp. 73–107, 2003.

[2] R. Altshuler and S. Newlon, "The effects of U.S. tax policy on the income repatriation patterns of U.S. multinational corporations," in *Studies in International Taxation* (A. Giovannini, R. G. Hubbard, and J. Slemrod, eds.), (Chicago), National Bureau of Economic Research, University of Chicago Press, 1993.

[3] T. Besley and M. Smart, "Fiscal Restraints and Voter Welfare," Unpublished paper, London School of Economics and University of Toronto. 2003.

[4] E. W. Bond and L. Samuelson, "Strategic behaviour and the rules for international taxation of capital," *Economic Journal*, vol. 99, pp. 1099–1111, 1989.

[5] G. Brennan and J. M. Buchanan, *The Power to Tax: Analytical Foundations for a Fiscal Constitution*. Cambridge University Press, Cambridge, 1980.

[6] M. Brückner, *Strategic Delegation and International Capital Tax Competition*. University of Bonn, 2000. Manuscript.

[7] S. Bucovetsky, "Asymmetric tax competition," *Journal of Urban Economics*, pp. 167–181, 1991.

[8] S. Bucovetsky and J. D. Wilson, "Tax competition with two tax instruments," *Regional Science and Urban Economics*, vol. 21, pp. 333–350, 1991.

[9] R. B. Davies, *The OECD Model Tax Treaty: Tax Competition and Two-way Capital Flows*. University of Oregon, Mimeo, 1999.

[10] J. A. De Pater and G. M. Myers, "Strategic capital tax competition," *Journal of Urban Economics*, vol. 36, pp. 66–78, 1994.

[11] P. A. Diamond and J. A. Mirrlees, "Optimal taxation and public production, I: production efficiency," *American Economic Review*, vol. 61, pp. 8–27, 1971.

[12] T. Dickescheid, "Exemption vs. credit method in international taxation treaties," *International Tax and Public Finance*, vol. 11, pp. 721–739, 2004.

[13] A. Dixit, "Tax policy in open economies," in *Handbook of Public Economics* (A. Auerbach and M. Feldstein, eds.), New York and Oxford, North Holland, pp. 313–374, 1985.

[14] J. Edwards and M. Keen, "Tax competition and leviathan," *European Economic Review*, vol. 40, pp. 113–134, 1996.

[15] W. Eggert and B. Genser, "Is tax harmonization useful?," *International Tax and Public Finance*, vol. 8, pp. 511–527, 2001.

[16] W. Eggert and L. Goerke, "Fiscal policy, economic integration and unemployment," *Journal of Economics*, vol. 82, pp. 137–167, 2004.

[17] W. Eggert and A. Haufler, "When do small countries win tax wars?," *Public Finance Review*, vol. 26, pp. 327–361, 1998.

[18] R. Elitzur and J. Mintz, "Transfer pricing rules and corporate tax competition," *Journal of Public Economics*, vol. 60, pp. 401–422, 1996.

[19] M. Feldstein and D. Hartman, "The optimal taxation of foreign source investment income," *Quarterly Journal of Economics*, vol. 93, pp. 613–624, 1979.

[20] B. Frey and R. Eichenberger, "To harmonize or to compete? That's not the question," *Journal of Public Economics*, vol. 60, pp. 335–349, 1996.

[21] C. Fuest, "The political economy of tax coordination as a bargaining game between bureaucrats and politicians," *Public Choice*, vol. 103, pp. 357–382, 2000.

[22] C. Fuest, "Economic integration and tax policy with endogenous foreign firm ownership," *Journal of Public Economics*, vol. 89, pp. 1823–1840, 2005.

[23] C. Fuest and T. Hemmelgarn, "Corporate tax policy, foreign firm ownership and thin capitalization," *Regional Science and Urban Economics*, vol. 35, pp. 508–526, 2005.

[24] C. Fuest and B. Huber, "Tax coordination and unemployment," *International Tax and Public Finance*, vol. 6, pp. 7–26, 1999.

[25] C. Fuest and B. Huber, "Labour and capital income taxation, fiscal competition, and the distribution of wealth," *Journal of Public Economics*, vol. 79, pp. 71–91, 2001a.

[26] C. Fuest and B. Huber, "Tax competition and tax coordination in a median voter model," *Public Choice*, vol. 107, pp. 97–113, 2001b.

[27] C. Fuest and B. Huber, "Why capital income taxes survive in open economies: The role of multinational firms," *International Tax and Public Finance*, vol. 9, pp. 553–566, 2002.

[28] J. J. Gabszewicz and T. van Ypersele, "Social protection and political competition," *Journal of Public Economics*, vol. 61, pp. 193–208, 1996.

[29] R. Gordon and J. K. MacKie-Mason, "Why is there corporate taxation in a small open economy? The role of transfer pricing and income shifting," in *The Effects of Taxation on Multinational Corporations* (M. Feldsteein, et al., eds.), University of Chicago Press, London and Chicago, pp. 67–91, 1995.

[30] R. H. Gordon, "An optimal taxation approach to fiscal federalism," *Quarterly Journal of Economics*, vol. 98, pp. 567–586, 1983.

[31] R. H. Gordon, "Taxation of investment and savings in a world economy," *American Economic Review*, vol. 76, pp. 1086–1102, 1986.

[32] R. H. Gordon, "Can capital income taxes survive in open economies?," *Journal of Finance*, vol. 47, pp. 1159–1180, 1992.

[33] R. H. Gordon, "Taxation of capital income vs. labour income: An overview," in *Taxing Capital Income in the European Union. Issues and Options for Reform* (S. Cnossen, ed.), Oxford University Press, pp. 15–45, 2000.

[34] R. H. Gordon and L. A. Bovenberg, "Why is capital so immobile internationally? Possible explanations and implications for capital income taxation," *American Economic Review*, vol. 86, pp. 1057–1075, 1996.

[35] R. H. Gordon and H. Varian, "Taxation of asset income in the presence of a world securities market," *Journal of International Economics*, vol. 80, pp. 361–375, 1989.

[36] L. Grazzini and T. van Ypersele, "Fiscal coordination and political competition," *Journal of Public Economic Theory*, vol. 5, pp. 305–325, 2003.

[37] T. A. Gresik, "The taxing task of taxing transnationals," *Journal of Economic Literature*, vol. 39, pp. 800–838, 2001.

[38] D. Hartman, "Tax policy and foreign direct investment," *Journal of Public Economics*, vol. 26, pp. 107–121, 1985.

[39] A. Haufler, *Taxation in a Global Economy*. Cambridge University Press, Cambridge, UK, 2001.

[40] A. Haufler and G. Schjelderup, "Corporate tax systems and cross country profit shifting," *Oxford Economic Papers*, vol. 52, pp. 306–325, 2000.

[41] A. Haufler and I. Wooton, "Country size and tax competition for foreign direct investment," *Journal of Public Economics*, vol. 71, pp. 121–139, 1999.

[42] A. Haufler and I. Wooton, "Regional tax coordination and foreign direct investment," CEPR Discussion paper No. 3063, 2001.

[43] J. Helliwell, "Benefactor's lecture," (Toronto), C.D. Howe Institute, 2000.

[44] J. R. Hines, "Taxation and U.S. multinational investment," in *Tax Policy and the Economy* (L. Summers, ed.), MIT Press, 1988.

[45] T. Horst, "A note on the optimal taxation of foreign source investment income," *Quarterly Journal of Economics*, vol. 94, pp. 793–798, 1980.

[46] W. H. Hoyt, "Property taxation, Nash equilibrium, and market power," *Journal of Urban Economics*, vol. 30, pp. 123–131, 1991.

[47] B. Huber, "Tax competition and tax coordination in an optimum income tax model," *Journal of Public Economics*, vol. 71, pp. 441–458, 1999.

[48] H. Huizinga and S. B. Nielsen, "Capital income and profit taxation with foreign ownership of firms," *Journal of International Economics*, vol. 42, pp. 149–165, 1997.

[49] E. Janeba, "Corporate income tax competition, double taxation treaties, and foreign direct investment," *Journal of Public Economics*, vol. 56, pp. 311–326, 1995.

[50] M. Keen, "The welfare economics of tax co-ordination in the european community: A survey," *Fiscal Studies*, vol. 14, pp. 15–36, 1993.

[51] M. Keen and H. Piekkola, "Simple rules for the optimal taxation of international capital income," *Scandinavian Journal of Economics*, vol. 99, pp. 447–461, 1997.

[52] P. J. Kehoe, "Policy co-operation among benevolent governments may be undesirable," *Review of Economic Studies*, vol. 56, pp. 289–296, 1989.

[53] J. Kennan and R. Riezman, "Do big countries win tariff wars?," *International Economic Review*, vol. 29, pp. 81–85, 1988.

[54] A. Kessler, C. Lülfesmann, and G. Myers, "Fiscal competition, redistribution and the politics of economic integration," *Review of Economic Studies*, vol. 69, pp. 899–923, 2002.

[55] H. J. Kind, K. H. Midelfart, and G. Schjelderup, "Why corporate taxes may rise: The case of economic integration," Paper presented at the CESifo Area Conference on Public Sector Economics, Munich, 9–11 May 2003.

[56] K. Konrad and G. Schjelderup, "Fortress building in global tax competition," *Journal of Urban Economics*, vol. 46, pp. 156–167, 1999.

[57] K. A. Konrad and K. E. Lommerud, "Foreign direct investment, intra-firm trade and ownership structure," *European Economic Review*, vol. 45, pp. 475–494, 2001.

[58] C. Leechor and J. Mintz, "On the taxation of multinational corporate investment when the deferral method is used by the capital exporting country," *Journal of Public Economics*, vol. 51, pp. 75–96, 1993.

[59] M. Leite-Monteiro, M. Marchand, and P. Pestieau, "Employment subsidy with capital mobility," *Journal of Public Economic Theory*, vol. 5, pp. 327–344, 2003.

[60] A. M. Lejour and H. A. Verbon, "Capital mobility, wage bargaining, and social insurance policies in an economic union," *International Tax and Public Finance*, vol. 3, pp. 495–513, 1996.

[61] K. S. Mansori and A. J. Weichenrieder, "Tax competition and transfer pricing disputes," Discussion Paper, University of Munich, Forthcoming in Finanzarchiv, October 1999.

[62] J. Mintz and M. Smart, "Income shifting, investment and tax competition: Theory and evidence from provincial taxation in Canada," *Journal of Public Economics*, vol. 88, pp. 1149–1168, 2004.

[63] J. M. Mintz, "Conduit entities: Implications of indirect tax-efficient financing structures for real investment," *International Tax and Public Finance*, vol. 11, pp. 419–434, August 2004.

[64] J. M. Mintz and H. Tulkens, "Commodity tax competition between member states of a federation: Equilibrium and efficiency," *Journal of Public Economics*, vol. 29, pp. 133–172, 1986.

[65] J. M. Mintz and H. Tulkens, "The OECD convention: A model for corporate tax harmonization?," in *Public Finance with Several Levels of Government/Finances Publiques avec Plusieurs Niveaux de Gouvernement* (R. Prud'homme, ed.), (Brussels), Proceedings of the 46th Congress of the International Institute of Public Finance, pp. 298–314, 1990.

[66] J. M. Mintz and H. Tulkens, "Optimality properties of alternative systems of taxation of foreign capital income," *Journal of Public Economics*, vol. 60, pp. 373–399, 1996.

[67] P. B. Musgrave, *United States Taxation of Foreign Investment Income: Issues and Arguments*. Cambridge, 1969.

[68] R. Musgrave and P. Brewer, *Taxation of Foreign Investment Income: An Economic Analysis*. John Hopkins Press, Baltimore, 1963.

[69] S. C. Myers and N. S. Majluf, "Corporate financing and investment decisions when firms have information that investors do not have," *Journal of Financial Economics*, vol. 13, pp. 187–221, 1984.

[70] W. H. Oakland and Y. Xu, "Double taxation and tax deduction: A comparison," *International Tax and Public Finance*, vol. 3, pp. 45–56, 1996.

[71] W. E. Oates and R. M. Schwab, "Economic competition among jurisdictions: Efficiency enhancing or distortion inducing?," *Journal of Public Economics*, vol. 35, pp. 333–354, 1988.

[72] OECD, *Model Double Taxation Convention on Income and Capital*. Report of the OECD Committee on Fiscal Affairs, Paris, 1977.

[73] T. Persson and G. Tabellini, "The politics of 1992: Fiscal policy and european integration," *Review of Economic Studies*, vol. 59, pp. 689–701, 1992.

[74] P. Raimondos-Moller and K. Scharf, "Transfer pricing and competing governments," *Oxford Economic Papers*, vol. 54, pp. 230–246, 2002.

[75] W. Richter and K. Schneider, "Taxing mobile capital with labour market imperfections," *International Tax and Public Finance*, vol. 8, pp. 245–262, 2001.

[76] W. Richter and D. Wellisch, "The provision of local public goods and factors in the presence of firm and household mobility," *Journal of Public Economics*, vol. 60, pp. 73–93, 1996.

[77] M. Sato, "Tax competition, rent seeking and fiscal decentralization," in *European Economic Review*, Forthcoming, 2001.

[78] H.-W. Sinn, "US tax reform 1981 and 1986: Impact on international capital markets and capital flows," *National Tax Journal*, vol. 41, pp. 327–340, 1988.

[79] H.-W. Sinn, "Taxation and the birth of foreign subsidiaries," Discussion Paper No. 90-30, University of Munich, 1990.

[80] J. Slemrod, "Free trade taxation and protectionist taxation," *International Tax and Public Finance*, vol. 2, pp. 471–489, 1995.

[81] P. B. Sorensen, "The case for international tax coordination revisited," *Economic Policy*, vol. 31, pp. 492–461, 2000.

[82] P. B. Sorensen, "International Tax Coordination: Regionalism versus Globalism," CESifo Working Paper 483, 2001.

[83] C. Tiebout, "A pure theory of local expenditures," *Journal of Political Economy*, vol. 64, pp. 416–424, 1956.

[84] A. Weichenrieder, "Anti-tax-avoidance provisions and the size of foreign direct investment," *International Tax and Public Finance*, vol. 3, pp. 67–81, 1996.

[85] D. Wellisch, *Theory of Public Finance in a Federal State*. Cambridge, 2000.

[86] D. E. Wildasin, "Interjurisdictional capital mobility: Fiscal externality and a corrective subsidy," *Journal of Urban Economics*, vol. 25, pp. 193–212, 1989.

[87] D. E. Wildasin, "Labor-market integration, investment in risky human capital, and fiscal competition," *American Economic Review*, vol. 89, pp. 73–95, 2000.

[88] D. E. Wildasin and J. D. Wilson, "Risky local tax bases: Risk-pooling vs. rent capture," *Journal of Public Economics*, vol. 69, pp. 229–247, 1998.

[89] J. D. Wilson, "A theory of interregional tax competition," *Journal of Urban Economics*, vol. 19, pp. 296–315, 1986.

[90] J. D. Wilson, "Tax competition with interregional differences in factor endowments," *Regional Science and Urban Economics*, vol. 21, pp. 423–451, 1991.

[91] J. D. Wilson, "Theories of tax competition," *National Tax Journal*, vol. 52, pp. 269–304, 1999.

[92] J. D. Wilson and D. E. Wildasin, "Capital tax competition: Bane or boon," *Journal of Public Economics*, vol. 88, pp. 1065–1091, 2004.

[93] G. R. Zodrow and P. Mieszkowski, "Pigou, tiebout, property taxation, and the underprovision of local public goods," *Journal of Urban Economics*, vol. 19, pp. 356–370, 1986.

Editorial Scope

Foundations and Trends® in Microeconomics will publish survey and tutorial articles in the following topics:

- Environmental Economics
- Contingent Valuation
- Environmental Health Risks
- Climate Change
- Endangered Species
- Market-based Policy Instruments
- Health Economics
- Moral Hazard
- Medical Care Markets
- Medical Malpractice
- Insurance economics
- Industrial Organization
- Theory of the Firm
- Regulatory Economics
- Market Structure
- Auctions
- Monopolies and Antitrust
- Transaction Cost Economics
- Labor Economics
- Labor Supply
- Labor Demand
- Labor Market Institutions
- Search Theory
- Wage Structure
- Income Distribution
- Race and Gender
- Law and Economics
- Models of Litigation
- Crime
- Torts, Contracts and Property
- Constitutional Law
- Public Economics
- Public Goods
- Environmental Taxation
- Social Insurance
- Public Finance
- International Taxation

Information for Librarians

Foundations and Trends® in Microeconomics, 2005, Volume 1, 4 issues. ISSN paper version 1547-9846 (USD 200 N. America; EUR 200 Outside N. America). ISSN online version 1547-9854 (USD 250 N. America; EUR 250 Outside N. America). Also available as a combined paper and online subscription (USD 300 N. America; EUR 300 Outside N. America).

Foundations and Trends® in
Microeconomics
Vol. 1, No 1 (2005) 1–62

Capital Mobility and Tax Competition

Clemens Fuest[1], Bernd Huber[2] and Jack Mintz[3]

[1] Center for Public Economics, Albertus Magnus-Platz, D-50923 Köln,
Germany, clemens.fuest@uni-koeln.de
[2] Department of Economics, University of Munich, Germany
[3] C.D. Howe Institute and University of Toronto, Canada

Abstract

This text surveys the literature on the implications of international
capital mobility for national tax policies. Our main issue for consideration in this survey is whether taxation of income, specifically capital
income will survive, how border crossing investment is taxed relative to
domestic investment and whether welfare gains can be achieved through
international tax coordination. Our analysis puts special emphasis on
multinational firms and the problem of financial arbitrage.

CPSIA information can be obtained at www.ICGtesting.com
Printed in the USA
BVOW011130231212

308908BV00002B/6/A